OVERTHINKING:

The Fast Cure for Women and Men Who Think Too Much and Want to Stop Procrastinating - Proven Tips to Turn Off Relentless Negative Thoughts in Place of Optimism and Strong Focus

By: David Drive

**Copyright © 2019 – David Drive
All rights reserved**

The content contained within this book may not be reproduced, duplicated or transmitted without direct written permission from the author or the publisher.
Under no circumstances will any blame or legal responsibility be held against the publisher, or author, for any damages, reparation, or monetary loss due to the information contained within this book. Either directly or indirectly.

Legal Notice:
This book is copyright protected. This book is only for personal use. You cannot amend, distribute, sell, use, quote or paraphrase any part, or the content within this book, without the consent of the author or publisher.

Disclaimer Notice:
Please note the information contained within this document is for educational and entertainment purposes only. All effort has been executed to present accurate, up to date, and reliable, complete information. No warranties of any kind are declared or implied. Readers acknowledge that the author is not engaging in the rendering of legal, financial, medical or professional advice. The content within this book has been derived from various sources. Please consult a licensed professional before attempting any techniques outlined in this book.

By reading this document, the reader agrees that under no circumstances is the author responsible for any losses, direct or indirect, which are incurred as a result of the use of information contained within this document, including, but not limited to errors, omissions, or inaccuracies.

Table of Contents

Introduction 1

Chapter 1: An Introduction to Overthinking & The Ways It Can Affect People 5
- What Is Overthinking? 6
- The Most Common Causes for Overthinking in Men & Women 11
- The Difference Between Overthinking & Being Prepared 14
- The Most Common Signs That Your Overthinking Is Controlling Your Behavior 16
- The Negative Effects of Overthinking 19

Chapter 2: What Is Procrastination & Why Is It Such A Difficult Habit to Break? 25
- What Is Procrastination & Where Does It Come From? 25
- Why Is Procrastination Such A Hot Issue When It Comes to Understanding & Conquering Overthinking? 30
- The Difference Between Habitual Procrastination & Poor Time Management Skills 32
- The Health Dangers & Other Negative Effects of Procrastination 35
- What Are Actions, Signs & Indicators of Procrastination in Men & Women? 40
- Procrastination Habits Identified: Now What Can Be Done to Help Fix Them & Solve or Come to Terms with the Issue as A Whole? 46

Chapter 3: The Causes & Stress Triggers That Lead People to Procrastinate 47
- What Causes Procrastination? 48
- What Kinds of People Are Most Likely to Become Procrastinators? 53
- The Connection Between Procrastination & Overthinking ... 56
- Use This Newly Gained Knowledge & Get the Answers You Have Been Searching For! 58

The Origins Have Been Explored. Traits Have Been Analyzed. What's Next for Breaking These Habits?.................... 60

Chapter 4: Taking Your First Steps (From Harmful Procrastination to Incredible Productivity) 62

The Baby Steps Method: All It Takes Is Two Minutes! 64
    Why This Method Works 69
    Who This Method Works Best For: 70

The Teamwork Method: Have Someone Hold You Responsible & Accept Their Help! 71
    Why This Method Works 72
    Who This Method Works Best For 73

When in Doubt, Get the App & Leave All of The Hard Work to Technology! 73
    Why These Apps Work 76
    Who These Apps Work Best For: 78

Take A Breather: Find a Fresh Perspective & Change the Way Things Look 79
    Why This Method Works 80
    Who This Method Works Best For 81

Chapter 5: To Overcome Overthinking, You Simply Have to Get Moving 83

Benefits of Breaking the Habit of Overthinking for Men & Women 85

The Most Important Step: Accept That No One Can Predict the Future or Change the Past 87

Walk on Sunshine: Embrace the Encouraging Influence of Positive Thoughts 89

Get Up, Get Moving & Be More Active 91

Invest in A Timer & Start Settings Limits for Yourself 93

Change the Way You Think: Gratitude Vs Regret 96

Think & Act with Confidence: Stop Asking "What If"? 99

Ask for Help: Reach Out to the People Who Love You & Build A Network of Support Around You 100

The Music Method: Take Control of Thoughts by Turning to Your Favorite Tunes 101
Meditation & Mantras: There's No Limit to Their Usefulness! 104
Get Out of the House & Volunteer: Turn Your Thoughts to the Needs of Others 106
The Conversational Exercise: Stretch Out All of Those Social Muscles & Skills 108
    Why This Exercise Works 110
    Who This Exercise Works Best For 110

Chapter 6: Confidence is Key When It Comes to Building Positive Habits 112

Self-Esteem & Confidence Levels: How Are They Connected & How Are They Different? 115
A Self-Awareness Exercise: Listen to Your Self Talk & Learn from What You Say 115
    Why This Exercise Works 118
    Who This Exercise Works Best For 119
What Is Self-Esteem? 119
    Where It Comes From 121
What Is Confidence (or Self-Confidence)? 122
    Where It Comes From 122
Why Are These Traits So Important for Men & Women to Embrace, Develop & Strengthen? 123
The Many Benefits of Building Self-Esteem & Confidence. 125
How to Get Started with Building Self-Esteem & Confidence Levels 127
A Self-Awareness Exercise: Get to Know Yourself & Your Restrictions 127
    Why This Exercise Works 130
    Who This Exercise Works Best For 131
Confidence Building Tip: Fake It Until You Make It 131
Check Who Is Around You: Surround Yourself with Positive People 133

How to Identify A Toxic Connection or Relationship.......... 134
Tips & Techniques for Shaking Toxic Relationships from
Your Life...138
Improve Your Own Self-Esteem by Helping Others Build
Their Own 141
Invest in A Journal & Create A Record of All of Your Forward
Progress 145
The Benefits of Keeping A Journal in Adulthood 147

Chapter 7: Moving Forward & Staying Strong in the Face of Every Challenge 152

Don't Let Others Determine How You View Yourself 154
Never Accept Failure & Always Plan for Success 156
If You Cannot Make A Solid Decision, Don't Be Afraid to Play
Devil's Advocate with Yourself 159
    Why This Exercise Works 161
    Who This Exercise Works Best For..............................161
Eat Right & Exercise: Turn Your Attention to Improving Your
Physical Health 162
If All Else Fails, Seek Professional Help & Support! 166

Conclusion 169

Introduction

Congratulations on choosing *Overthinking: The Fast Cure for Women and Men Who Think Too Much and Want to Stop Procrastinating!* In doing so, you have taken the very first step on the path from overthinking and procrastination to improved productivity and glowing self-confidence. This helpful guide was designed to be not only informative and educational but also fun to read and encouraging to everyone who is ready to learn the best ways to start making positive changes in every part of their life from personal connections to professional reputation.

In the following chapters, the guide will discussand provide helpful details on subjects including and connected to habitual overthinking and how to overcome it, such as:

- Common negative side effects and health conditions that have been tied to psychological habits like procrastination and overthinking
- The connection between procrastination and overthinking
- Benefits and other positive effects people have experienced after overcoming their habitual psychological compulsions
- Detailed explanations of what habitual overthinking is and what it is not so that readers can better understand where these types of psychological habits come from
- What causes overthinking and procrastination habits to develop and how to identify their origins to better design an action plan for conquering them

Throughout the course of the guide, readers will also learn about factors and variables involved with the development of overthinking and procrastination habits like:

- What kinds of people and personality types are more likely to develop overthinking and procrastination habits
- How to create personal mantras or start meditating in order to gain better control over one's emotions and stay motivated during times of doubt or lack of energy
- How to improve communication and become more emotionally open with the people they trust to create an encouraging and supportive network
- Helpful activities, tips and tricks for increasing their own self-esteem and becoming more confident in anything they do
- How to stay focused and determined on the path toward their goals, regardless of their current emotional state or unexpected complications and challenges that may arise throughout the course of this personal adventure toward an improved life!

By the end of this educational and informative guide, our hope is that readers are more confident in themselves, have more faith in their own abilities and feel ready to not only conquer their negative psychological habits, but any challenges or mountain that has stood in their way but seemed impossible to master before. Within this guide are the skills, basic facts and most cutting-edge methods and techniques that every person can use to reach their personal improvement goals, regardless of their individual factors and variables.

We know that there are no shortage of self-help guides and other books of this nature on this subject on the market and every effort was made to ensure it is full of as much useful information as possible. Thanks again for choosing this one and congratulations again on getting started toward a more mentally, physically and emotionally healthy lifestyle! Good luck on your journey and please enjoy *Overthinking: The Fast Cure for Women and Men Who Think Too Much and Want to Stop Procrastinating.*

Chapter 1: An Introduction to Overthinking & The Ways It Can Affect People

We are lucky to live in a time where it is not just scientists and medical professionals that are able to earnestly understand and learn to adjust how the human mind works. Since the acceptance of psychology as a valuable and respectable form of health science, massive amounts of information have been collected and studied by experts all over the world in order to better understand human thoughts, behaviors and actions and how they are shaped by the psychological variables that each individual faces throughout their personal life paths.

There are a seemingly endless number of psychological concerns people can face, but one of the most commonly experienced and reported across the globe is overthinking. While many people find ways to cope with their personal overthinking struggles so that it does not take too much control over their lives, there are also many out there who end up seeking help after missing out on opportunities, distancing themselves from personal relationships and other negative impacts that can come from the inability to take action because of habitual overthinking.

What Is Overthinking?

The definition of overthinking is typically listed in the simplest terms as "thinking about something for too long". While the definition makes it seem like something that is easy to understand and obvious to recognize, the habit itself is much more complex and damaging, particularly when experienced over long periods of time without understanding or relief.

Specifically, habitual overthinking is different for each person and can come with a variety of variables and negative effects that will also be different for each person. The key to discovering the causes and origins for each person's individual overthinking habit comes with a focus on self-awareness which includes the individual being more aware of not only their current emotional state during times of overthinking, but also:

- Their emotions regarding the events, subjects or responsibilities they are overthinking about
- Any common factors between different overthinking sessions
  - For example, some people may notice that they only have difficulty overcoming their overthinking habit when they are stressed or under unusual pressure at work. Others may notice that their overthinking sessions are focused around someone in particular and the individual's previous or upcoming interactions with them.
- Their thoughts and actions in similar situations in the past (if there have been any similar situations) and what they learned from that experience
- Any other particular variables like the number of people they are working with on a specific issue, recommendations they have received from others trying to help ease their current

situation or emotional state and all tasks, resolutions or responsibilities that are included in their current concerns

Rarely do I ever have a

by itself.

It's more like:

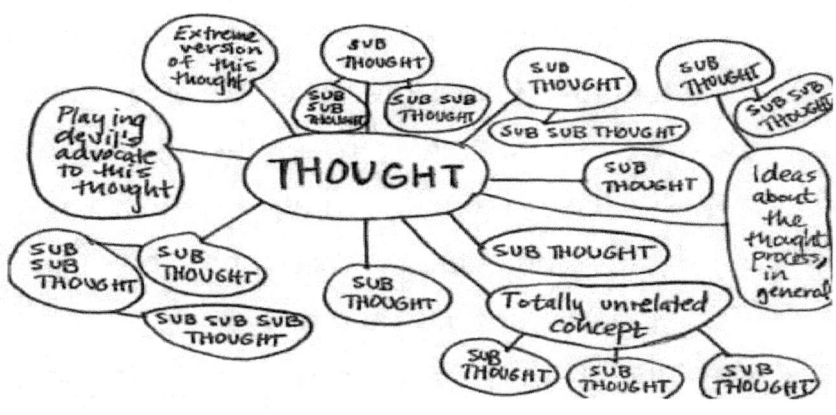

In psychological terms, overthinking is not just thinking about something for longer than is required, recommended or accepted as normal. The main reason for this is because everyone has their own ways of thinking about things and every subject, option, opportunity or question comes with a variety of variables that can determine how long something needs to be contemplated or what needs to be considered before taking action, such as:

- How many choices the individual has to make to come to a solution
- The urgency or importance of the subject
- How many other people may be affected by their potential decisions or actions
- Pros and cons or risks and benefits related to the subject

Just thinking about overthinking can be enough to inspire anxious responses and impulses in people, especially those who struggle with overthinking as a psychological habit. These people are set apart from those who fall into the leadership category with their organization, strategy and readiness because their overthinking does not lead to efficiency or productivity. Their thinking never stops- with options, risks, rewards, involvement and any other number of variables spinning around in their thoughts without ever leading to helpful or successful action.

For those who have never experienced it, overthinking and its various negative effects can be difficult to explain or understand. In fact, in many cases, describing what overthinking *isn't* is more effective than trying to describe what it is.

What overthinking is *not*:

- A conscious decision that can just be stopped on command
    - Overthinking is a psychological impulse, often a response to anxiety, that becomes habitual over time
- An unbreakable habit or impossible to overcome
    - There are lots of steps and actions people can take in order to change the way they think about and approach different situations
- Something to be taken lightly as it can be damaging emotionally and psychologically over time
    - People who suffer from habitual overthinking often have other psychological issues that affect their ability make a solid decision and move

forward with it without regret or increased levels of stress
- A disorder on its own
    - Overthinking can be controlling and dominant for those who struggle with it, but in the end, it is caused by a larger psychological concern and not a disease or disorder by itself

What overthinking *is*:

- A symptom of a larger psychological concern that leads to an inability to take action when faced with decisions or responsibilities of varying urgency or importance

The Most Common Causes for Overthinking in Men & Women

It's connection to previous experiences, environmental influences and situational variables can make it difficult to pinpoint specific causes of overthinking in individuals. However, recent studies have shown that there are several common causes and factors reported in men and women around the world.

One of the most common causes that has given scientists and doctors insight into overthinking is a as an indicator or sign of psychological disorders such as Post-Traumatic Stress Disorder (PTSD), various anxiety disorders and various phobias. Anxiety disorders are the most prevalent in today's society, many believe that it is due to the overstimulation from technology (televisions, advertisements, radios, and all of the handheld devices that media can be carried around and played on). For those with anxiety disorders, the overthinking comes with a more intense version of anxiety known as meta-anxiety, which is a stage of anxious behavior in which an individual is getting anxious about their own anxiety and the potential for panic attacks or similar episodes in the near future.

In some cases, and often those not related to psychological issues, the cause for this type of overthinking is related to a lack of self-confidence, self-esteem or questioning one's own abilities with regards to the subject or problem at hand. Some of the most reported overthinking experiences described by study subjects in this category include:

- Fixating on things that should or should not have been said after the event, situation or issue has been resolved
- Comparing themselves to others at work, school or whatever specific environment in which they will have their performance observed or appraised
- Assuming the worst before, during and after a situation that leads to anxious behaviors, a feeling of uncertainty and a vulnerability that causes overthinking

Overthinking is often an emotional response in some people whenever they are faced with an important task or decision they need to make. It begins with a knock to their self-esteem as they worry about their ability to accomplish what has been asked of them. This doubt in themselves leads them to feel poorly about the task or subject from the very start and only increases the impulse to overthink in most people. Since the individual in this example is already doubting themselves and their abilities, they are now faced with the fear that others will see it in their results or solution and from here their mind can take a few different actionable paths including overthinking or procrastinating. Overthinking happens more often when someone feels the need to prove themselves through their task while many turn to procrastination in an effort to distract themselves from their concerns regarding their responsibilities.

The Difference Between Overthinking & Being Prepared

Most people know at least one person who is always prepared for anything that comes up or at least has the appearance of control and organization. In some cases, this may be the individual themselves. The ability to maintain control (or the illusion of control) in any given situation, particularly when others involved are giving in to the stress, is a valuable talent and a developed skill that is commonly sought after in leadership and management roles.

It is not only those with psychological conditions that are prone to overthinking. It is one of the most common complaints for adults living in the 21st century who find themselves hesitating or needing a break from their current environment in order to clear their minds enough to make a solid plan or decision. At some point in their life (often many times throughout), every individual finds themselves overthinking or ruminating about something that they should be able to let go of or move on from. This is a natural response as humans related to our survival instincts and need to have control over situations. Since people cannot see the future, it is natural desire for everyone to be as prepared as possible for any situation that arises.

One of the most common excuses for people trying to avoid facing their issues with overthinking in their daily lives is to claim that they are not overthinking but being cautious, thorough or paying attention to detail in order to set themselves up for success. This could be for minor inconveniences or encounters throughout their daily routines or for larger, more stressful or emotional issues that do require consideration and caution before coming to a conclusion.

If there are times, situations or concerns that require more thinking than others, how is it possible to tell when someone is taking their time to make sure they are coming to the best decision and when someone is just habitually overthinking? Unlike much of what is known about overthinking, this answer is simple:

- People who are taking their time to make solid decisions they are confident in and won't come to regret will take action or announce their decision when they have considered all of their options and concerns.
- People who are overthinking will run through all of their options and concerns only continue run through their thoughts until it evolves from being thorough to becoming obsessive. These people will never take action or announce a decision, preferring the repetition and safety of their own thoughts until someone else eventually takes control, withdraws their offer or makes a decision on their behalf.

The Most Common Signs That Your Overthinking Is Controlling Your Behavior

Before steps can be taken to ease and even eliminate habitual overthinking, it is important to know whether or not you (or someone you are concerned for) is overthinking as a matter of psychological impulse related to anxiety or fears, or if overthinking is a sign of a larger issue that needs to be explored and addressed. Here are some of the most common warning signs and indicative behaviors that those who are prone to damaging overthinking habits exhibit, especially when put under pressured or faced with a new task.

Pessimism: One sign that many overthinkers tend to overlook (or fail to accept) is their tendency to assume the worst in any given situation. Claiming to be a realist and not a pessimist is a common assertion with overthinkers in denial about their issue, but the truth is that overthinking and the negative psychological and emotional symptoms connected to it grow to pollute the way individuals see the world around them. Hope and excitement for life are replaced with anxiety and fear of change leading to a completely negative view of the world around them that can be difficult to see beyond.

Repetition: One of the main descriptions used by those trying to explain what overthinking feels like is circling or whirling thoughts in their mind. No matter where a thought starts, what logical path it follows or what other thoughts it ends up inspiring, those who are overthinking and unable to take action find their thought process right back at the beginning where their initial concerns and thoughts evolved from. Once overthinkers have reached the point where actions or decisions should be initiated, followed all of their related thoughts through their logical paths and have nothing else to obsess over, instead of making their move, they will just go back to the beginning and start the overthinking process all over.

Inability to Move Forward: People who overthink about things (from encounters with other people to opportunities they have taken or passed up) have very little confidence in their own ability to make the right decision, regardless of the situation. It can be something major like deciding to take one job over another or something small like whether they said or did not say something they should have when they spoke to someone new at the coffee shop. For various amounts of time (sometimes years) after a particular event or meeting, habitual overthinkers will replay everything that was done or said, questioning every point of concern and their vocal or actionable responses to them. Even if nothing came from the subject in question or there is nothing that can be done to change any related events that followed or continue around them, people who overthink will continue to relive the scenario until something else becomes more stressful or urgent for them to worry about.

Too Inwardly Focused: One of the causes for overthinking in people is the fear that comes with social interactions or maintaining relationships, both personal and professional. This fear causes people, particularly those who are also prone to expecting the worst, to worry over every word they exchange or even how their facial expressions are interpreted by those they encounter on a daily basis. These people can often have issues with empathizing or focusing their thoughts on others, making come across as anti-social or even unpleasant. This is not always the case though. There are many overthinkers that maintain healthy social interactions without regret or concern dominating their thoughts after each night out or lunch with friends. It is all a matter of how self-aware an individual is, how developed their emotional intelligence is and how in control they are over their habitual overthinking or procrastinating impulses.

The Negative Effects of Overthinking

For those who are concerned for themselves or for others they know are struggling with getting control of their overthinking habit, knowing the negative ways overthinking can affect both the mind and body is a good way of waking up even the most stubborn of friends and family. While not everyone who deals with overthinking will experience all of the connected effects discussed in this chapter, here is a closer look at some of the most prevalent and widely experienced negative effects caused or aggravated by habitual overthinking.

Absence of Inner Peace: Since overthinking is often connected to anxiety and stress-related impulses, one common negative effect is a persistent and inescapable feeling of negativity that can manifest as a number of traits such as:

- Depression
- Pessimism
- Reclusiveness
- Disinterest in being social (even with close relations like family or romantic connections)

For people who overthink, this habit does not just affect their decision-making abilities. It can spread to affect all aspects of their life, leaving a negative impact wherever it touches. Since they are always worried about what is happening around them, it is often impossible for overthinkers to find their emotional center or any kind of psychological stability that brings peace and relaxation throughout their mind and body.

Physically & Mentally Exhausting: One negative effect overthinking has on people is that it consumes and burns away energy from the mind and body that could be used more effectively. People who struggle with habitual overthinking typically also suffer from mental and emotional burn out, constant or regular fatigue and tend to get sick more often than those around them (whether it is at work, home or both).

Respond Emotionally to Situations That Do Not Call For It: Another negative effect overthinkers face is that over time, they lose their ability to respond rationally or logically to statements others make to them or situations that are purely professional. Whether it is getting excessively or unreasonably defensive about comments, observations or criticisms made to them or having emotional breakdowns in situations that do not require it. Habitual overthinkers spend so much time and energy focusing on the hypothetical or repetitive thoughts whirring around their minds that when they are faced with minor inconveniences or unexpected interruptions (especially if they require immediately responses or actions).

Warped View of the World Around Them: Arguably, the most damaging effect of overthinking is that throughout the years and as individuals struggle through their personal challenges, overthinkers start to believe the things they tell themselves during their episodes of overthinking. This would not be as concerning if people focused on positive and encouraging thoughts when they were overthinking, but the harm in overthinking comes from centering one's thoughts on negative subjects or events and replaying them in their mind until nothing else is able to break through their thoughts. This can warp people's view of the world in a number of ways like making them assume that everyone they encounter is thinking negatively about them or that everything they say is being criticized or obsessed over the same way they obsess about them when overthinking. The more someone focuses on thoughts like these, the more they become the automatic response to new encounters or unfamiliar surroundings. When these thoughts become normal for someone, they become difficult to break free from and start to affect all aspects of their lives so that soon, even events or situations that should be enjoyable take on a negative tone as the individual overthinks about how each person around them is thinking about them and whatever they are (or are not) doing.

Less Social & More Inclined to Separation: People who spend massive amounts of their free time (or times they are supposed to be focused on other, more productive habits or tasks) have very little time to spend with their friends and family. The main reason for this is that they are too consumed by their cyclical and repetitive thoughts about regular social situations and experiences like what other people think about them, analyzing each and every word they say or wish they had said, and coming up with hypothetical encounters to prepare themselves for imaginary conversations that may never take place. In many cases, the stress of all these thoughts and pressures becomes overwhelming and the individual decides it is best to just stay home and get lost in their favorite television shows or whatever activity they take part in within the safety and protection of their own home and private space.

In addition to all of these concerns, overthinking is also the most commonly recognized negative effect connected to procrastination in men and women of all ages. While a dangerous psychological habit on its own, overthinking becomes even more restrictive and harmful when paired with habits like procrastination.

Chapter 2: What Is Procrastination & Why Is It Such A Difficult Habit to Break?

The definition of procrastination is widely accepted as the act of delaying or avoidance of an action or decision. While this definition is accurate, as with the definition of overthinking, it is also overly simplistic when trying to understand procrastination as a psychological concern. It is a major factor and common practice for those who also struggle with controlling their tendency to overthink.

What Is Procrastination & Where Does It Come From?

More than just a popular word in the English vocabulary, procrastination is a negative habit that has existed and been recorded since the early days of humanity. Most prevalently connected with a Greek poet named Hesiod, one famous view of the human impulse to procrastinate was published "work prospers with care; he who postpones wrestles with ruin". In fact, the word "procrastinate" originally comes from the Latin term *procrastinare* which translates into "put off until tomorrow". The psychological theory connected to the word "procrastination" comes more from the early Greek phrase *akrasia*, a word which means to do something against one's better instinct or judgment.

This is a repetitive theme amongst procrastinators regardless of location, situation, age or experience: even while they put off their responsibilities, they know that there will be consequences to face if they are not able to get it done in time or by when it is expected to be resolved. However, this knowledge is not enough to inspire action or decision, instead only serving to fuel the procrastination habit by putting the individual in a deeper and more tumultuous emotional state that only continues to strengthen the urge to hide from their current situation. As their deadline or time limit grows ever closer, they begin to remember their real-life responsibilities and consequences and panic sets in. Now they fully realize the amount of work or the weight they needed to get done or the weight of the decision they needed to make begins to weigh heavy on their shoulders. They rush to get everything completed and come to a solution for the situation they've been procrastinating with. In many cases, they are unable to complete it and have to face the real consequences such as having to work off the clock or having to request an extension, their dedication to their position called into question by their superiors. In some cases however, procrastinators are able to get everything completed and instead of having to regret their decision to procrastinate, they convince themselves that they do their best work under such pressures and the habit is born.

Other famous sayings related to procrastination (and the importance of handling it efficiently) include:

- Don't put off until tomorrow what you can do today- Benjamin Franklin
- While we waste our time hesitating & postponing, life is slipping away- Roman Philosopher, Seneca

The first quote is intended to help individuals reach their full potential by inspiring them to take more control over their actions and get themselves moving today. This may work for some as a personal mantra or a reminding poster on their office wall, but for those who struggle with procrastination as a compulsion and as a habit, quotes like Mr. Franklin's have very little effect. Seneca's quote on the other hand (and the poem that it comes from) serves to remind individuals that procrastinating does nothing but waste time and energy that could be spent on other activities like trips they could be taking with the extra time or promotions they could be working towards with the extra energy once their avoided tasks are finished.

One of the most common misconceptions connected with procrastination is that it is a matter of laziness or lack of discipline on the part of the individual, but the truth is that procrastination has nothing to do with how much self-control a person has. In this chapter, we will cover the finer details of procrastination and reveal some surprising facts about the condition and how it affects men and women of all ages.

The following cartoon and pie chart provides a solid visual of what it is like to be victim of your own overthinking by someone else who has experienced and wrestled with overcoming their own psychological struggles. Through this simple visual presentation, it is easy to see how overthinkers tend to spend their time and the regret that comes with not having the skills of knowledge of how to take control of their thoughts and behaviors.

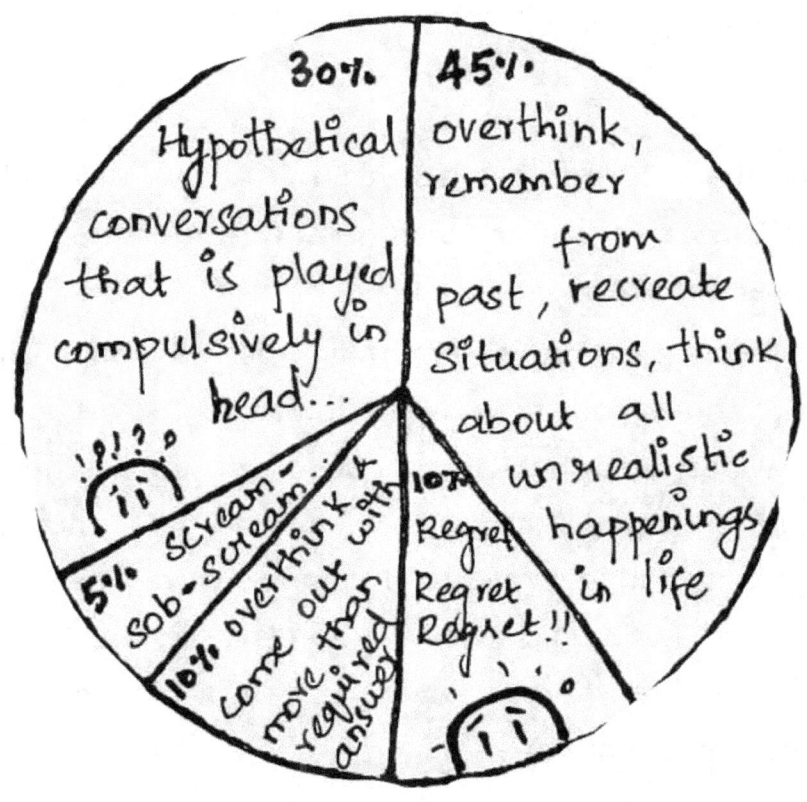

Pro Tip: Art is a great way analyze and process difficult emotions of thoughts about anything! It exercises the creative part of the brain which helps with emotional control and strengthening over time. Using art as a means of emotion and thought processing in place of obsessive or compulsive overthinking gives individuals a unique, productive and effective way of expressing their personal thoughts, desires, goals, fears and any other factors or variables they are looking for help with understanding and controlling.

Why Is Procrastination Such A Hot Issue When It Comes to Understanding & Conquering Overthinking?

Procrastination is something that all adults wrestle with throughout their lives. However, just because it is a widespread habit, that does not mean that it is natural or healthy for those who find themselves procrastinating regularly or compulsively. The negative side effects (which we will be discussing later in this chapter) can take a severe toll on a person's mental and emotional health. One of the main reasons for this is because the majority of people looking for answers on how to beat their procrastination have enough psychological self-awareness to know how unproductive and hindering the habit can be. They can see how behaviors like procrastination and overthinking are holding them back from reaching their full potential and even with this knowledge, they are unable make themselves take any action or make any solid decisions. This knowledge throughout each of their procrastination processes eats away at their self-esteem, causing them to feel even worse and more stressed out as their deadline approaches or the pressure they are under continues to increase.

It isn't just the mind that feels the effects of procrastination over time. In fact, the long-term negative effects of this habit can be damaging not only psychologically and emotionally, but it can also affect people physically as stress levels (and the physical body processes connected to stress like blood pressure levels and breathing speed) fluctuate into unsafe regions. This fluctuation and inconsistency can lead to muscle weakness (especially in the heart) and even blood clots in more extreme cases.

Many psychological professionals are taking an interest in procrastination and overthinking as serious health concerns with some even going as far as to categorize them as self-harm behaviors. These types of behaviors and related habits are getting more and more attention as depression, anxiety and suicidal numbers increase across the globe. The more information that is gathered and studies that are performed on habits like overthinking and procrastination, the more society as a whole will be able to understand the difficulties related to these types of conditions and the more solutions can be found for those who have had trouble finding the answers they need for their specific concerns.

The Difference Between Habitual Procrastination & Poor Time Management Skills

One criticism that procrastinators often hear is that they would not be as stressed or pressured in life if they knew how to use their time better. While this seems like a logical solution to a problem that is notorious for burning energy and letting time pass inefficiently, but when it comes down to it, poor time management and procrastination are not the same issue.

Those with poor time management skills have a much easier path ahead of them when it comes to stopping the delay or avoidance of their responsibilities and replacing it with better and more productive habits. This is because in many cases, their poor time management impulses come from a lack of knowledge about how best to prioritize or organize their time to reach their most efficient and productive level. Once these individuals learn the necessary skills they require in order to take control of their time management behaviors, they may find themselves procrastinating from time to time, but now it is not related to their inability to see the problem as a whole or come up with a plan to accomplish their goals in an effective and reasonable time frame.

Procrastination is different in that many people who are aware that they struggle with procrastinating in various aspects of their life are also aware that they possess the time management skills that should be helping them through every episode of procrastination.

Pro Tip: Take the time to analyze your own behaviors or the behaviors of someone you are concerned is struggling with procrastination. If there are tasks they come across that they can get planned out or put together with little to no additional stress, then this is a good sign that this person already has effective time management skills. However, if they then avoid taking actions or making any kind of starting motion on their plan, then this person is most likely having difficulty overcoming their habitual procrastination.

- If the person being analyzed is you, then you have already made a major accomplishment in conquering your procrastination habit: accepting the issue as reality and recognizing the damaging behaviors that make it such a concerning habit.
- If you are concerned about someone else's habitual procrastination or lack of time management skills then the best course of action once you have identified their particular behaviors and habits is to speak openly with the person about your concerns. This conversation may help them see the problem in a new light, knowing that others have been able to see it as well, which may also help them to understand and accept the challenge they are facing. Like with any trial or challenge, there is no way to help someone change their ways (even if it would be the best course of action for them) until they are willing to admit, accept and begin to learn about their condition and where it comes from.

Those who are unwilling to accept their habitual procrastination often do so because they are not currently under stress, are feeling fine or are in a positive frame of mind. In this type of mental state, procrastinators are able to justify their actions or push them to the back of their mind until their mood starts to slip to the more negative end of the spectrum and the overthinking spiral starts.

The Health Dangers & Other Negative Effects of Procrastination

There are as many different types of effects and dangers associated with procrastination as there are different types of personalities. While some may be common or at least reported in various different situations and studies, each person has their own struggle and individual variables that cause and fuel their procrastination so not every person will experience each of the different negative effects in a way that makes a lasting impact (or at all).

Loss of Time: One of the most obvious negative effects of procrastination is the amount of time that is allowed to just pass or be burned on unproductive tasks. Some people say this is not directly connected with procrastination but with a person's time management skills (a disconnect that many psychologists are supporting as studies show that procrastination and poor time management skills are not necessarily the same issue or even connected in some cases). There are those procrastinators that are lucky enough to have enough trivial tasks or things that they've been meaning to do to occupy their procrastination time but those who do not spend this time searching for something to do to appear productive so that they can justify their procrastination to their logical selves in some way.

Loss of Energy: Many may see procrastination as a form of laziness, but the truth is the amount of energy it takes to procrastinate is often more exhausting on the mind and body of the individual than just doing their task or making their decision would have been. Instead of just getting done what they need to finish, procrastinators spend massive amounts of energy on anxious behaviors such as pacing or waste energy up at night overthinking about their responsibilities and how they need to get them done, keeping the person from getting any sleep to restore the energy that they're wasting on the stress and panic that comes with procrastination.

Track Record of Bad Decisions: Procrastinators often struggle with regret and obsess over past decisions during their episodes of overthinking that only make them feel worse about themselves and their abilities over time. When people doubt themselves, they become less concerned with thinking about their options or trying to plan things out because they lose hope and begin to believe that anything they chose to do will end poorly so why bother putting time and energy into weighing options. When decisions are made in this mind set, people are not concerned with potential consequences, figuring any path is full of them so just pick one and roll with the punches. Their low self-esteem leads to lack of hope, motivation and passion over the years. This behavior can also become habitual over time and people who are not concerned with the benefits or consequences of their actions have very little chance of building a successful future for themselves.

Damage to Reputation: This could be professionally or personally as one behavior often associated with procrastination is making promises or plans only to break or cancel them at the last minute. Professionally, this could ruin someone's career if allowed to get out of hand. Personally, many people who wrestle with procrastination impulses have ended up alienating themselves from friends and loved ones by avoiding or skipping social situations.

Long-Term Negative Health Risks: The stress and sleeping issues that affect procrastinators are just some of the ways procrastination damages people's health. Individuals that struggle with procrastination in their personal and professional lives are more inclined to letting the habit seep into other aspects of their life such as exercising and going to the doctor. The exercising skipping as a habit starts innocently enough, typically with the individual missing a regular session or a planned lesson for a reasonable circumstance. Sometimes this circumstance or change may be out of the person's control. The issue is not that they have missed the one workout, the issue is that everything was okay while they missed that one exercise window, in fact, they may have felt better that day than they normally do after exercising because they are not all sore and sweaty. This positive feeling they remember the next time they don't feel like exercising at their regular time or skipping their lesson and the procrastination habit takes control.

Adults should attend regular annual check-ups to ensure their health and always check in with their doctors when health concerns are starting to worry them. Procrastinators often avoid going to the doctor under nearly any circumstance and others may make appointments with the best intentions only to skip them when the time comes. One of the most repeated excuses for procrastinators with this habit is that they feel fine in the moment and that the appointment is just time that could be used on the task or responsibility they have been procrastinating on. Using their favored reasoning or justification, they talk themselves out of getting their check-up or going to see their doctor, cancelling their appointment often never to reschedule it until there is an emergency or their loved ones hold an intervention.

Other negative health effects that have been linked to habitual procrastination include:

- Heart damage, particularly for individuals already at risk of heart disease for lifestyle or genetic reasons
- Inconsistent sleep patterns that lead to mental and emotional stress and burnout throughout the day

- Damage to emotional health and wellbeing with continuous trials and suffering of the emotions and psychological processes on an individual as they try to beat or justify their procrastination tendencies

Once procrastinators see the health risks and potential dangers associated with habitual procrastination, many are more likely to be willing to start taking steps toward taking control of the impulses and psychological compulsions that are commonly practiced with their condition. Now that we've covered the health risks, keep reading for a closer look at some of the most common warnings signs and indicative behaviors seen in procrastinators of all ages.

What Are Actions, Signs & Indicators of Procrastination in Men & Women?

While procrastination is widespread phenomenon amongst adults of all ages, races and locations, it is not a healthy habit (as we discussed above) and one that is difficult to break once it has reached a point that the individual is experiencing more negative effects than benefits to their procrastination practice. The good news for procrastinators everywhere is that with some patience and practice, anyone can stop procrastinating and start living up to their full potential! One way to accomplish this is first by checking for warnings signs or indicators in oneself or others to determine whether they are a habitual procrastinator or just someone who struggles with time management.

They Are Often Distracted: Those who fall into the category of habitual procrastinators often struggle in social situations as they tend to be distracted, looking for topics, conversations or activities they can take part in to avoid whatever task or responsibility they are procrastinating with.

One of the most prevalent indicators of a procrastinator is the habit of searching for distractions. These are the more active procrastinators that are unable to talk themselves into getting a specific task done but is also have trouble with letting time pass without productivity. These types of procrastinators will often make lists of other tasks they have been meaning to get done or less important tasks that they can convince themselves they will be able to knock out quickly so they can focus all of their attention on the one main issue or subject. Their past experiences with procrastination and the negative side effects they've had to deal with will tell these types or procrastinators that they are setting themselves up for unnecessary stress or even failure, but the compulsion to avoid tasks or make decisions is more powerful than their logical thoughts.

They Are Often Overwhelmed By A New Task or Assignment: Procrastination is a habit directly tied to emotional and psychological impulses, factors and desires, depending on the individual. This is why many habitual procrastinators can overreact or give into rising feelings of panic or frustration whenever they are presented with a new responsibility, tasks or opportunity. Even if it is something that will affect them in a positive way, either through the process of completing in or once the activity or solution in question is reached, many procrastinators only see the negative side of it: more work, something else to do, another decision *they* are going to have to make or another plan *they* have to come up with. Whatever an individual's specific reasons or excuses, their first reaction to new situations is often an emotional one triggered by stress and fear that affect their thoughts and behaviors in ways that make them difficult to work with or even be around, depending on the situation.

They Have Difficulty Dealing with Unexpected Changes or Disruptions: One thing procrastinators are often good at is making plans for what they need to get done within their specific time frame. In most cases, it is the only way for them to be able to justify their procrastination because they know they have a solid plan of action laid out and prepared for when they are ready to get started. This plan of action is often their only comfort and fallback when the panic from time constraint or pressure starts to take its toll and they begin to regret their procrastinating.

This is why when unexpected difficulties, tasks or decisions arise, procrastinators often have difficulty emotionally or logically handling the change because they most likely did not plan any spare or free space in their time frame for anything to go sideways or come up. Planning additional time is not something that procrastinators think about, although it is a time management skill that many adults already possess. It is an invaluable part of organization and preparation for any task that many people make sure to leave room for as fear of the future and the uncertainty that something could disrupt even the best laid plans are natural human reactions.

They Have a Bad Habit of Showing Up Late: Whether it is to work, class or social events, habitual procrastinators are often known in their professional or social groups as the person who is most likely to show up not only late, but most likely unprepared for whatever it is they are facing that day. This bad habit leads to a reputation of unreliability that can damage someone's professional and personal relationships or connections.

This known habit of being late regardless of consequence or importance gives procrastinators a disadvantage when it comes to building their futures as it gives them a reputation for being unreliable that can penetrate all aspects of their life from their professional responsibilities to their social, familial or romantic relationships. Since they are always late, or at least late often enough that others have begun to notice or remark on it as a regular behavior, they are not as trusted as their peers or other members of their group and can often alienate themselves over time or start to get left out of events and gathers since the people they would be going to see may have started to just assume the individual would be bailing anyway. It is not just personal relationships that can be affected. Their superiors may observe this habit of being late and see it as a weakness in their employee, that person then finds themselves missing opportunities or getting passed up for projects or assignments that could further their standing or career.

They Focus on Trivial or Non-Essential Activities Before Getting Their Necessary Tasks Completed: Another one of the most common traits displayed by habitual procrastinators is a strong reliance (even a dependence) on lists and organization, regardless if it is at home or work. The lists themselves can range in length or priority but are typically filled with smaller tasks or lighter decisions that the individual may have been thinking about for some time, but that he or she is using as a means of distraction from the more pressing tasks they are procrastinating with.

The only thing about these lists is that while they may be informative and impressive when looked at on first glance, but if someone were to investigate how many of those tasks have actually been marked off or even started, they would be highly disappointed. Despite their lists, their preparation and their organization, most procrastinators never end up checking off their entire lists, or even the majority of them. Of course, this varies from person to person and how out of control their procrastination impulses are, but it is one of the few behaviors that most habitual procrastinators share as it gives them viewable proof to use against or wave at people who question their productivity.

Procrastination Habits Identified: Now What Can Be Done to Help Fix Them & Solve or Come to Terms with the Issue as A Whole?

The first step in finding a solution to any problem is to understand how it starts, where it comes from and how it connects to overthinking. While many people may find the cause of their procrastination is similar to others working to conquer with the same matter, every individual will have their own variables and specific situations that may set them on a different path to understanding and overcoming their personal struggle. Keep reading, as these are topics we will cover thoroughly in the next chapter!

Chapter 3: The Causes & Stress Triggers That Lead People to Procrastinate

Coming to terms with procrastination and overthinking starts with finding out where they come from. As with any psychological issue or concern, the answers regarding origins and what lifestyle points might affect them will be different for each individual. Fortunately, modern psychologists and health professionals have spent plenty of time studying these behavioral phenomena and the amount of knowledge related to overcoming them has grown exponentially in the last few decades.

Through various studies and surveys, professionals across the globe are discovering and sharing their findings with regards to who is most at risk for developing psychological habits, how to identify them and how they can be treated. As with any medical or health-related topics, not all symptoms and traits are going to be true for every person who struggles overthinking or procrastination habits. The point of gaining this knowledge is to determine which factors or variables each individual is facing so that a plan can be formed for how best to tackle their personal situation.

Now that we've provided a better understanding of what overthinking and procrastination are, let's take a closer look at where they come from and what types of personalities are more likely to cave to their emotionally driven psychological compulsions.

What Causes Procrastination?

If procrastination is something that everyone has to deal with at multiple points throughout their life, can it really be all that bad? Despite the many health and well-being risks associated with habitual procrastinating and overthinking, there are still those who refuse to believe that their personal habits and compulsions are under control and far from being dangerous to their mind or body.

Pro Tip: This denial is one of the challenges all people wanting to take control of their habits and behaviors must overcome before any forward progress can be made. If someone is unwilling to acknowledge their issue and make a conscious decision to change, then they are not going to be able to improve their behaviors or psychological habits.

However, there is plenty of hope and proven techniques out there that have made all the difference for those wanting to give up procrastinating and overthinking. The most recent studies have shown that the development of habitual procrastination can be traced back to four main psychological causes:

- **Unable to Focus or Gain Control of Thoughts:** Sometimes people who have difficulty with controlling their thoughts or getting themselves to focus have their behaviors being controlled by their emotions rather than their logical thoughts. Emotions are truthful and powerful, but they are also unpredictable and capable of changing without warning, especially for those with existing psychological conditions.

- **Fear of Failure & Fear of the Unknown:** These are perfectly natural phobias that every person faces at some point in their life. While for many the fear disappears once a plan has been made or more information has been gathered, but for others these types of fears (which can be encountered in nearly any given situation) can lead to full-blown panic attacks and other emotional reactions can affect their behavior and inspire psychological habits like procrastination and overthinking to take control of all thought and action.

- **Lack of Motivation & Low Levels of Energy:** These two traits are often connected as many who find themselves trying to cope with procrastination also have experience with larger psychological concerns like depressive states, suicidal behaviors in extreme cases, and the development of anti-social behaviors related to lack of confidence or faith in their own talents, abilities or future potential. This negative thinking constantly circling through their mind can leave damage on an individual's self-esteem, a negative emotion that comes with physical side effects such as fatigue, low immune system efficiency and muscle soreness throughout the body with little to no physical strain to cause it.

- **Need to Reach Perfection:** This is a common trait that comes with the fear of failure and is one of the main causes of procrastination. Through their previous experiences with procrastination and their tendency to overthink, they begin to believe that the only way they will be able to complete something or come to a proper resolution is if their application is totally flawless. Of course, perfection is an often impossible bar for people to reach, particularly when distractions, interruptions and unwelcome challenges can arise at any time and throw off even the most well-planned solutions.

There are still those out there that argue habits like procrastination and overthink cannot be nearly as harmful as people claim they are since everyone deals with them at some point but not everyone falls prey to their control of behaviors and reactions to situations throughout life. Recent studies have looked into this fact as well as determined that the reason not everyone develops dangerous psychological habits because there are those in the population that are more susceptible to the negative and long-term effects than others.

In the following comical chart, it is easy to see the type of distracting thoughts and actions people take when avoiding their tasks and responsibilities, along with the fluctuations in stress levels that come with giving in to habitual procrastination.

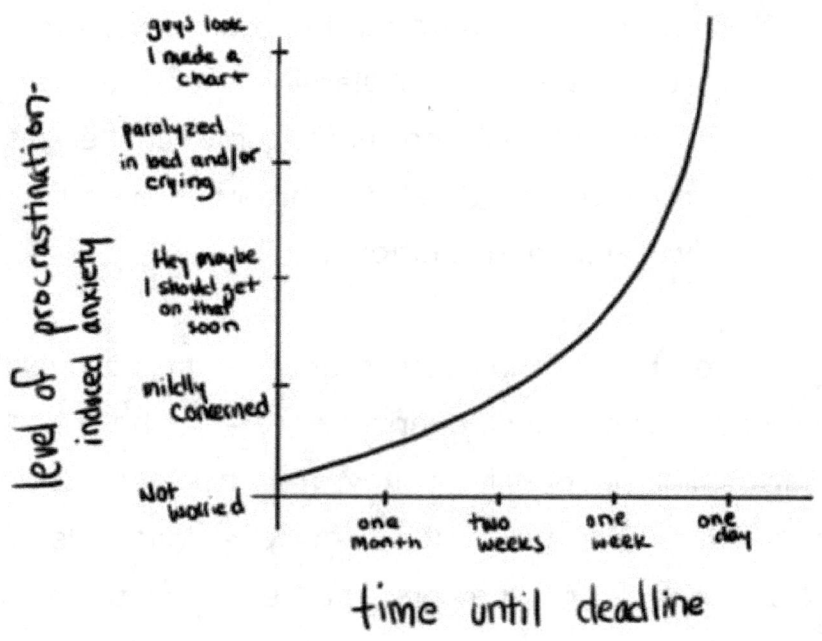

While the image itself may have a comical tone, it is an accurate and widely relatable visual of the types of thoughts that dominate someone's mind when procrastination habits have control over a person's mind, emotions and behaviors.

What Kinds of People Are Most Likely to Become Procrastinators?

Like with all psychological habits and behaviors there are some with different personalities and lifestyle variables that can be more or less likely to develop procrastination or overthinking habits. Some of these common variables and personality types include:

Perfectionists: People who struggle with being a perfectionist often also have difficulties controlling their impulse to procrastinate. One of the main reasons for this is because people who take pride in perfection and faultless execution in everything they do are less concerned with not getting a task done than they are finishing something that is flawed in any form. However, for many procrastinating perfectionists, the closer their deadline comes or the higher the pressure gets for them to take action, the more panic sets in an they find themselves in a panicked frenzy to complete their task.

Students: Students, regardless of age or education level, are some of the most common victims of procrastination and overthinking. One of the reasons for this is often connected to a lack of confidence in their own talents and abilities that causes them to obsess about each and every detail of their assignments until they are trapped in a whirlwind of thoughts that keeps them from completing their task. Another one of the main reasons for student procrastination is the self-deception that comes with the belief that they perform better under the pressure of a nearly impossible deadline. Despite being told over and over by their friends and family that they will not only feel better, but that the quality of their work will improve if they didn't procrastinate, the impulse is too strong in many cases and the need to put off their responsibilities takes over.

Pro Tip: Those who use this excuse are able to convince themselves that they will be able to complete their task to their best ability even in the shortened amount of time typically because they have done it before. It only takes one successful event for the habit to start and take control. The first time someone procrastinates and is still able to complete their task or find their solution in time for someone to start procrastinating as a matter of habit and compulsion.

People Pleasers: Those who find themselves constantly surrounded or often outnumbered by people who are difficult to please often become procrastinators. These types of people are eager for those around them (both peers and superiors) to see them in a certain light. It could be that they lied or fictionalized something about themselves in order to paint this picture for their friends or co-workers, or it could be that there is no reason for the person to feel inferior to those around them because they are just as experienced or talented, but do not see it because their self-esteem has been so wrecked by their procrastinating and overthinking habits.

Those Who Have Learned Through Experience: Those who procrastinated until they were under the gun and managed to come out on top without consequence once or twice by accident are more likely to develop a problem with habitual procrastination because their experience has taught them that they are still able to put out quality work or make solid decisions without having to spend the effort and energy on the time management skills and patience it would take to achieve their goal in a timely and comparatively stress-free manner. While they may consider themselves lucky at first, the longer this habit is allowed to develop and is practiced by the individual, the further the quality of their work and performance (often in various aspects of their life) will slip until those they work or interact with take notice and action.

The Connection Between Procrastination & Overthinking

While the two are often symptoms of a larger psychological concern that should be acknowledged and explored, habitual procrastinating and overthinking have also been linking as being the cause for one another. Overthinkers who consider themselves driven and motivated in everything they do find that over time, their psychological habit of obsessing over small interactions or replaying regrets through their mind can develop into habitual procrastination over time as these individuals try to find ways to distract themselves from their dominating thoughts and emotions, often pushing aside responsibilities or pressing tasks to avoid having to think about them.

Alternately, those who start as procrastinators may find over time that they are overthinking more and more about the things happening around them, personally and professionally. One of the main reasons for this is that those who are self-aware enough to recognize their impulse to procrastinate in matters from choosing where they want to eat dinner to delivering a major presentation to their employers are also emotionally intelligent enough to realize that the anxiety and panicked emotions that come with that habit are only increasing their stress and decreasing their chances of success. Unfortunately, although they are aware of their habitual procrastinating and overthinking, the compulsive behaviors associated with those habits are more powerful than rational thinking and are often determined by how the individual is feeling at any given moment. This only makes the habitual overthinking worse as it brings up questions like why the person can't just make themselves take an action or make a decision and why they start procrastinating every time they face something, knowing how much stress, regret and guilt comes with the process.

Another connection that is common between the development of procrastination and overthinking habits is a third psychological stage that is fueled by emotions like the fear of failing and the awareness of passing time and burning energy that could be used more productively. This stage is an overwhelming guilt that also comes with negative health and wellness effects like fluctuating stress levels and uncertainty of one's ability to accomplish anything.

Use This Newly Gained Knowledge & Get the Answers You Have Been Searching For!

After the last few chapters, we hope you're feeling better informed and more confident in your knowledge of overthinking, procrastinating and where they come from. Now that the knowledge has been collected, it is time to put it to use and start preparing for those first steps forward with taking control of your mind, behaviors and emotions in order to conquer your habitual overthinking and/or procrastination.

As with any plan, the first step is to take a step back and analyze the situation as a whole. Answer these questions about yourself or the person you are concerned for to get a better read on the big picture and the individual factors that may affect treatment:

- What behaviors have you noticed that could be connected to habitual procrastination or overthinking?
- What is the individual's personality type? Do they fall into the category of higher risk personalities?
- What specific factors could be causing the habitual procrastination or overthinking?
- Are there certain situations where their behaviors, thoughts and actions (or lack thereof) can be identified as compulsive or driven by emotion rather than rational decisions?
- Have you (or the individual in question) acknowledged and accepted that there is a problem with these habitual compulsions that is hindering their ability to function at their full potential?

The Origins Have Been Explored. Traits Have Been Analyzed. What's Next for Breaking These Habits?

Now that the foundation has been laid for better understanding of psychological concerns like procrastination and overthinking habits and information has been shared about who is statistically most likely to develop these habits over others, it is time to start making an actionable plan for how to change the way the mind thinks and views the world so that impulses like procrastination and overthinking lose their power over your behaviors. Answer the following questions to determine whether or not you are prepared to begin taking control of your mental and psychological health in order to improve the health of your whole being:

- Have you fully acknowledged your individual negative psychological habit or multiple habits?
- Are you prepared to make conscious decisions and alterations to your behaviors and reactions?
- Can you stick to these changes, overcoming your emotional impulses that may arise and challenge your determination?

- Are you ready for a better life packed with as much fulfillment, success and discovery as you can fit into each day?

If the answers to these questions are all *yes*, then it is time to get started and time to take control of any and all psychological behaviors to make the most of life and everything it has to offer! Congratulations on gaining the knowledge and preparing yourself for the first steps to overcoming overthinking for a less stressful and more efficient life at home, work, school and/or any other situations where you find emotional responses and irrational behaviors setting the pace for you. In the chapters to come, we will be discussing tips, tricks and the most cutting-edge techniques in use around the world today from some of the most trusted and respected professionals and experts in the field!

Chapter 4: Taking Your First Steps (From Harmful Procrastination to Incredible Productivity)

There is not one easy solution when it comes to finding the best way to conquer one's habitual procrastination. The main reason behind this is that procrastination comes in varying urgency levels. For some people, they are only experiencing the compulsion to skip, shrug or put off their responsibilities in this moment but may have had no trouble getting things done on any other day. This type of procrastination is often connected to the person's current emotional state. Perhaps they have had a bad day or are fatigued from a lack of sleep the night before, and often times giving in to the procrastination habit is not as dangerous and may even be the best option for their mental and emotional health. This type of procrastination is not habitual but rather inspired by unusual circumstance.

PROCRASTINATION FLOWCHART

For others, their procrastination is something they have to battle with every time they have set a goal for themselves, have a deadline to meet or an obligation to fulfill. This type of procrastination is more damaging as it becomes habit easily, a habit that is widely accepted as one of the most difficult to break. The good news for people with this type of procrastination struggle is that there have been people around the world searching for and perfecting different methods and techniques, tips and tricks for how to overcome procrastination for those with the motivation and determination to get started!

As you have read, there are so many different origins and variables that can give a procrastination habit its power within a person's mind. Since there are so many different variations, it only makes sense that there are just as many different courses of action that can be taken in the quest to overcome procrastination. In this chapter, we will be covering (in detail and with as much information as possible) the most proven, practiced and professionally recommended methods for beating habitual procrastination available today!

The Baby Steps Method: All It Takes Is Two Minutes!

One popular method making its mark on the psychological and business communities is the *Baby Step* or *Two Minute Method*. With this method, people are able to lay the foundations and start taking action toward breaking their procrastination habit and building positive habits in its place.

This method confronts and tackles procrastination habits head-on with actionable plans that begin with taking a step back from the individual's problem or task, analyzing it and listing the steps to completion from the simplest to the most difficult or time-consuming, depending on the person's priorities. Once the situation has been analyzed and broken down into its simplest and most basic steps, the person needs to make a plan of action for their task and list each step they need to take from the beginning to the resolution.

The trick to mastering this method is that each step should take no more than two minutes to complete.

If the different stages of the task become too complicated to complete in two minutes and the person is not in a situation where they are not procrastinating, then the next step of this method is to break each of the remaining, more complicated steps down into two minute tasks and continue to do so until the entire task is completed their satisfaction. It may sound more complicated in explanation than it is in practice, so here is an example to provide a clearer picture of the Baby Steps Method in action:

- Someone has been trying to finish a manual for a new work program that are going to have to start using regularly next week. Their procrastination has told them that they have plenty of time (seven whole days) before they have o have the manual completed so they don't need to worry about it now.
    o Potential Situation A: The person listens to their procrastination thoughts and doesn't touch the manual until five days have passed. Now the panic begins to set in as they realize they now have 48 hours before

they're supposed to have the manual completed. From here, there are two main courses of action:

- The person can grab the manual and skip everything they had planned for the next two days in order to dedicate the entire amount of time to making their way through the manual before work starts again in 48 hours.
- The person can become overwhelmed by the pressure and end up just skimming or flipping through the manual to try and collect as much information as possible in order to improvise or "wing it" when they get to work and have to start the new program.
- In either of these situations, the individual is putting themselves at a disadvantage, either because they have had to cancel plans with friends and family, put off errands or chores they needed to get done, or just gone in blindly to a situation that can have a

serious impact on their productivity, success and quality of work.
- The Baby Steps Method: Instead of putting off reading the manual until later in the week, the individual looks at how many pages there are or how many chapters or sections there are and splits them up evenly over the seven days they have to complete the manual before work starts again. This way, they have just set their first goal for the task: reading a little bit each day to help with content absorption and stress control.
  - Now that the goal has been set, they have a rational plan that they understand carries the most benefits for them. The challenge now is to not let their procrastination habit start to whisper in their ear when the time comes to start their reading each day that it is not that much if they wanted to skip their reading goal one night. The rationalizing behind this is that they still have tomorrow and that the additional section is not that much to make up.

- When thoughts like this start to take over, the next step is look back at the basics of the task, in this case, getting the section of the manual read for the day.
  - What is the first thing a person needs to do if they want to get something read? Pull out and open the manual. Once this task is completed, it will be easier and feel more natural to start reading.
  - Once the manual is open, the next step is to get the reading started. The next step is to then get one complete page read.
- At this point, the person is more likely to keep reading until they reach their daily goal because they have already done the hardest part: pulled out the book and started reading.
- Even if the person decides to stop reading and play catch-up with their reading tomorrow, they can still take pride in having made a forward and

positive step toward conquering their habitual procrastination.

Why This Method Works: The reason the Baby Steps Method has proven so effective for men and women around the world is that it is based on the positive reinforcement of actionable behaviors, instead of focusing solely on the negativity of the procrastination habit. The purpose of the Baby Steps Method has little to do with the procrastination behavior itself and instead gives the individual the skills they need to master the practice of showing up. What this means is that even though there are times where the habitual procrastination will come out on top in the struggles, but as long as the person has taken the first of their two minute steps and completed it (and hopefully more of their two minute steps in the process), then they have already made progress on overpowering the habit by simply showing up and beginning the goal they set for themselves as opposed to completely avoiding any positive action.

There are a number of reasons why people who are using the Baby Steps Method should still feel good about their progress, even in the situations where they complete each of their two minutes steps and the procrastination still takes control:

- Habits are not built or broken in one try! It takes practice and dedication to stop procrastination and replace it with efficient and productive habits.
- Procrastinators often have reputations for breaking promises, cancelling plans and showing up late to important events or responsibilities (if they show up at all). By learning to just take some kind of action toward their smaller goals, they are learning how to show up and the more they are able to practice that skill, the more it will start to positively affect their behavior in other aspects of their life where procrastination has kept them from showing where and when they are supposed to.

Who This Method Works Best For: This method works for anyone who is looking to start a new habit or build a positive behavior in place of one they are trying to break free from. Those who have habitual procrastination habits will benefit from this practice in any aspect of their lives and will see the most progress over time.

The Teamwork Method: Have Someone Hold You Responsible & Accept Their Help!

From the dawn of time, humans have always proven stronger when working together than trying to survive on their own. The Teamwork Method uses this base instinct between humans to band together in a way that helps with breaking their bad habit in a way that they are also receiving the support and encouragement of the people around them. At its basic level, the Teamwork Method involves:

- Analyzing the task, responsibility or action that needs to be completed and design a plan of action from start to finish.
    - If there is a deadline or date when everything needs to get done, then do not forget to include it in the plan during this step.
- Once the plan has been made, the person then shares it with one to five people who they trust to keep them on task when they get distracted

or to offer positive support when they start to shirk their responsibilities.
- o This could be friends or family who already know about their issues with procrastination and want to help. These people could also be others who are involved in the task or subject the person is working on.

Why This Method Works: People are more likely to meet their responsibilities and reach their goals when they know that others are counting on them or cheering them on. When a person shares their goals with people they trust and people they respect the opinion of, they build a network of positive energy that they can call upon whenever they are feeling low or unproductive. That positive reinforcement helps to boost them up and keep them motivated throughout their trials and challenges.

Pro Tip: The most important part of mastering this method is free and open communication between friends, family or co-workers and anyone else included in the person's support team. Those who struggle with asking for help or have difficulty sharing how they are feeling or what they are thinking even with those they are closest to will not find this method effective for improving their lifestyle and breaking their bad habits.

Who This Method Works Best For: Those this method will work best for those who have already been open with the people they trust about their struggles and are ready to not only ask for help, but to accept it when it is offered. Even if someone has difficultly with open communication, if that is something they are working on along with overcoming procrastination or any other positive changes they are trying to make, then they will be able to work on that with this method as well as those who have already mastered or are already pleased with their communication skills.

When in Doubt, Get the App & Leave All of The Hard Work to Technology!

For those who are not great communicators or do not have the support network that others may have, there are still options for getting control of those psychological compulsions! One of the most popular options in today's technology driven society is to download an app and get started with virtual scheduling programs and personal assistants. Depending on the individual's specific needs and challenges, there are a variety of apps available for androids and iPhones that can help! Here is a more detailed look at some of the most popular apps available now:

- **1-3-5 List:** This app was designed to target those who find that their habitual procrastination is most closely linked to their difficulty with prioritizing their tasks. With this app, users choose a number of tasks they are hoping to complete each day: one large, three medium and five smaller tasks that need to be completed, actions that need to be taken or decisions that need to be made. Once these various goals and responsibilities have been entered into the program, the app helps the user prioritize and plan the order in which to complete the tasks so that they make the most out of their time and energy each and every day!
- **Simple Habit:** This app was designed for those who have heard about the ease and health benefits connected with meditation and have wanted to try it for themselves but have not yet started. This could be because of

simply not knowing where or how to start, or because it is one of the big concerns they have been procrastinating with. This app is perfect for those who find their procrastination is connected closely with the pressure stress or performance anxiety that comes with having to complete a task, make a decision or attend an event and function in a social situation. With easy and pressure free meditation sessions available in a variety of time intervals, anyone can find a meditation track that targets their specific needs. In addition to offering a variety of programs, this app also personalizes meditation recommendations based on the user's individual preferences so that it is most productive and effective over time.

- **Mindly:** This app works best for those whose procrastination habits are tied to their difficulty with getting focused and organized. Many apps rely on to-do lists and other organization methods that work best for linear minds. Instead, this app connects related thoughts, events, responsibilities, tasks and goals in interconnected circles that allows the user to move around and organize anything on their mind from things they have to do and when they are do to things they want to accomplish and how long they are hoping that will take. This is app has proven invaluable for those who are better able to stay organized or focus their mental tracks in a way that creates a picture or that allows them to visualize to suit their best preferences.

Why These Apps Work: These apps work by keeping track of an individual's responsibilities, events or deadlines and sending them regular reminders (that can often be controlled and timed to fit the person's preferences) in order to keep their task or project in the front of their mind. By keeping their goals in the front of their thoughts, more people see success in getting started and staying focused or motivated in situations similar to those they have had difficulty managing before. These apps work best by not just focusing on breaking the procrastination habits, but also helping to increase the user's overall productivity, whether it is in personal or professional settings.

One of the other reasons these apps are so productive for some people is that they are for those who like to take action and just need help focusing their energy or their thoughts on tasks at hand. Another benefit of working with these apps is that different apps are designed to target different variables that can contribute to a person's individual procrastination habits. Some apps can target multiple variables such as scheduling, notification reminders and communication options. Others focus on just one for those who have targeted their main issue and are looking for a tool to help them gain control over it.

Pro Tip: Not all of these apps are free. Some of them have a use fee or a monthly subscription. If they offer a free trial then that is the best way to start, but for those who are serious about breaking their procrastination habit and find during the trial that the app if helping with their struggle, then the price might be worth the reward. However, if you do try an app (free trial, with a temporary subscription or just by diving in with both feet to give it a shot), and find that you are not using it as much as you thought you were or that it is not helping as much as you had hoped, do not continue to pay for it! There are so many different methods and options available for conquering procrastination that

Who These Apps Work Best For: These apps are designed for people who do not have issues with procrastination due to lack of motivation or need for perfection. Instead, they are designed to help with organization, scheduling, communication reminders and keeping lists. They are designed for people who procrastinate because of the sheer number of things they have to do, those who find themselves overwhelmed by everything being asked of them. Whether this overwhelming pressure is coming from one current situation or is a consistent and regular matter of a busy lifestyle, these apps can help by working as a virtual personal assistant.

Pro Tip: One of the downsides to these apps is that most of them only work if the individual enters the deadline, information and other details they need to have in order to achieve their goal into the app's scheduling or assistant program. If a person downloads that app but is unable to stay on top of entering their tasks and action plans, then the apps will not help with their personal psychological habits and just take up space on their phone.

Take A Breather: Find a Fresh Perspective & Change the Way Things Look

One simple step for those who get anxious when trying to make changes or overcome their more dominant impulses is to get out of their current surroundings. Whether it is getting up to stretch and take a short walk around the room or in more extreme cases, taking a weekend trip to visit a friend or family member, finding somewhere else to think about and plan out your responsibilities or tasks can make all the difference in coming up with a logical resolution instead of giving in to procrastination habits or other negative psychological impulses.

Not taking an annual vacation or even taking some time off to support one's personal physical, emotional and mental health is one of the most common issues facing adults in the 21st century. This is another major cause of anxiety and high levels of stress in men and women of working age across the globe. In some cases, a person's psychological habits such as procrastination are a direct result of not having any personal time to relax or ruminate on their own health. Adults become so focused on building their careers and getting those promotions that they become fatigued and even exhausted, physically and mentally. Over time, this lack of support for personal health takes its toll on a variety of factors such as motivation and quality of work.

Why This Method Works: There are experts in just about any field (medical, private or professional) across the globe that will testify to the benefits of taking a step out of one's current surroundings in order to gain a fresh perspective. There are an endless umber of health and wellness benefits like overall emotional status improvement for those who find that the stress of their jobs or their home situation is the cause of their procrastination habits and overthinking.

Planning for vacations (or even for just taking a mental health day off from work and other pressures) gives people something to look forward to. That alone is often enough to help individuals feel more positively about the tasks the need to complete, plans they need to design, solutions they need to come up with and decisions that need to be made in the days or weeks between their current emotional state and the time their break starts. Positive people have better control over their emotions and a more confident understanding of their thoughts and feelings regarding stresses and pressures that their procrastination habit is trying to encourage them to avoid.

Who This Method Works Best For: This method is beneficial for everybody, regardless of the intensity or dominance level of their habitual psychological compulsions. During surveys and interviews, experts interested in the development of anxiety, negative psychological habits and related subjects found that the majority of people could not remember their last vacation, the last time they took some time off for their personal physical or mental health, or even regularly take breaks that are required by law or recommended by their employer.

Pro Tip: If there is not one single method, tip, trick or technique that makes a difference for your specific concerns or getting control of your psychological habits, design your own plan that focuses on your specific hopes and goals! Combine effective methods and abandon those that you have tried without any noticeable success. Never be afraid to ask more questions, seek out more information and pull together from multiple sources to form the most effective, inspiring and successful plan you can! The trick to mastering this technique is to stay organized and not be afraid to share with others what you are doing and how you are feeling in order to keep focused and motivated throughout your personal experience.

Regardless of where someone's personal struggle lies or where it comes from, there is some kind of action or path that they can start with in order to overcome their habitual procrastination. It just comes down to finding the right information and getting together the drive and motivation to take the first steps!

Chapter 5: To Overcome Overthinking, You Simply Have to Get Moving

Similar to procrastination, overthinking is a psychological habit that does people more harm than good over time. As a compulsion and emotional response to stress, overthinking is not something that people can just stop doing by simply wishing it into being. It takes work, effort, dedication and above all, planning! Before the anxiety or stress starts to kick in, there is a wide range of action plans and proven steps that people can take to put an end to their overthinking. This mean that no matter what factors cause or enflame the overthinking habits, individuals can find a solution that works for their situation and helps them to take control of their mind and thinking process in a way that is effective, productive and successful! In this chapter, we will we going into detail for some of the most tried, tested and recommended options for those ready to take control of their thoughts and stop falling prey to the dangers of overthinking.

Pro Tip: Before choosing or designing a specific plan of action, the first step overthinkers need to take is to increase their self-awareness, psychologically, emotionally and mentally. The more self-aware someone can be in the moment, the more control they will be able to maintain over their thoughts, actions and behaviors in situations that put pressure on them. People who are more self-aware are also better able to live in the moment which means that they have less regrets about the things they say and do (or do not say and do, depending on which variables are causing them the most stress and increasing their impulse to overthink).

Benefits of Breaking the Habit of Overthinking for Men & Women

Overthinking has a lot of potential negative side effects that can damage the mental, physical, emotional and psychological health of any individual. For those who are tired of having to deal with these negative effects and make positive changes in order to break their overthinking habit, there are a number of benefits to get excited about! Some of the most widely reported and talked about for men and women of all ages include:

- One of the most encouraging benefits of not overthinking regularly includes a more improved ability to live in the moment. Instead of thinking about past regrets or worrying about things that may never come to pass, people who do not spend their time and energy on overthinking are more involved in what is happening around them and better able to form strong and lasting connections with the people they interact with regularly or may not see all the time but care about and want to be better about communicating with.

- People who do not overthink tend to be better leaders and supervisors because they are able to make decisions based on thought and logical instead of emotionally or in a panic as many who suffer from habitual overthinking have to deal with. Even if management is not their goal, their self-motivation that comes with the confidence and pride in their own abilities means that people who are able to beat their overthinking habit into submission are better able to reach their goals, no matter what they are because they are not distracted by constantly circling negative thoughts and the damaging effects that come with those thoughts.
- For most, their anxiety is the cause of their overthinking, but there are also those who find that they do not have issues with anxiety until their overthinking habit kicks in. Those who have discovered a connection between their anxiety and their habitual overthinking (regardless of which causes the other) see positive changes and unexpected benefits when they make the conscious decision to get control over their overthinking. By developing

the skills needed to change their thoughts, emotions and the way they think about things, people who find effective ways to conquer or cope with their overthinking habits become better able to control their anxiety in other aspects of their life.

These are just some of the benefits that come with finding a way to beat habitual overthinking! Each person has their own reasons for wanting to stop and their own benefits they are hoping to experience when they do achieve this goal. Keep reading to learn more about those methods, tips and techniques that can help people with both their overthinking habits and personal anxiety concerns.

The Most Important Step: Accept That No One Can Predict the Future or Change the Past

One of the main causes of overthinking in men and women all over the world is the fear of what is unknown and the fear of what cannot be predicted. Another is the loss of control that comes with obsessing over past events or encounters that in hindsight could have been handled been or more to a person's personal satisfaction.

The first step to stopping overthinking and all of the negative effects that come with it is to understand that there are things that no one can see coming and that there will always be things we think could have been handled better or that we wish we could change, and then accept these thoughts as fact. Once these facts have been accepting, the sense of freedom that most people feel is enough to get them through their difficult times and move forward from getting their thoughts stuck in a repetitive cycle that becomes habitual overthinking. That freedom and the positive emotions that come with it help with motivation and staying on track when people hang on to those good feelings and call on them when situations start to become difficult or overwhelming.

Until these facts are understood and embraced, no one will be able to successfully get control of their habitual overthinking. Like with those who are concerned for others but have not been able to help because the person in question is unwilling to acknowledge that they have an issue. Without the self-awareness and acceptance of the unknown, overthinkers will continue to get lost in negative thought cycles and the become victim to their dangerous and negative side effects.

Walk on Sunshine: Embrace the Encouraging Influence of Positive Thoughts

One trait that many overthinkers share is that they focus on the negative aspects of their tasks or situations and what can go wrong over what can go right or how the person can benefit. They get some overwhelmed by issues that can arise, negative effects their actions or words may have, and any other bad factors and variables that could mess up their plans or decision process. What many overthinkers do not realize is that these negative thoughts are the most powerful fuel behind their habitual overthinking and until they find a way to see the world around them or process what happens around them in a more positive light, they will not be able to get the best of their habitual overthinking.

Many will dismiss this behavior as being prepared for anything or as their being a realist instead of being naïve. However, there is a big difference between positivity and naivety. Those with a positive demeanor or view of the world are better able to control their emotions in stressful situations because they are more practiced at finding rational and thoughtful solutions to their problems or challenges instead of caving to emotional responses fueled by negative thoughts and feelings about their current situation. Those who are naïve are often described as being positive to the point of delusion. They hold on to their positive thoughts and feelings regardless of whether or not their individual situation needed a stricter or more confident course of action. They deny negative emotions and push them aside instead of finding a way to deal with them. This action is only further damaging their mental and emotional health while strengthening their compulsion to give in to their habitual overthinking instead of facing negative situations.

People who focus on positive thoughts are able to acknowledge and react reasonably to negative emotions that arise in their different interactions and responsibilities. These types of people are more energized, better at socializing and typically more driven in their tasks because their mind is not burdened with stressful or painful thoughts that they are unable to break free from the repetition of.

Get Up, Get Moving & Be More Active

One of the best techniques in practice for those looking to stop their habitual overthinking is to get the blood pumping and find a way to get moving! Overthinking tends to happen most frequently when people have nothing else to occupy their thoughts productively. It is during those down times, or in those times when the person is looking for a distraction (like those who also struggle with procrastination as a habit), that people start to ruminate about past actions or possible issues they expect in the future. That is why most people report that the majority of their overthinking begins in places like the shower or while they are waiting for their ride and becomes the most dominant in their thoughts around bedtime as they try to fall asleep (or when have difficulty falling asleep).

One change people make when trying this method for overcoming their habitual overthinking is picking up a new habit! Preferably this habit is one that gets either the mind or the body active and distracted from repetitive, stressful thoughts that kick off the overthinking sessions. Increased blood flow, air flow and muscle stretching are all physical benefits involved with most extracurricular activities and they also have psychological benefits like improving focus and boosting positive energies.

For some, they may have better luck with an artistic or creative habit like taking a painting class or going out and getting involved with their community theater. For others, this habit could be more focused on physical fitness and activities. Some people may take this opportunity to start a regular exercise routine like going to the gym for a set amount of time two to three times a week (maybe even with extra sessions when their overthinking gets really out of control). For others, this could be an opportunity to try an activity they have always wanted to learn but never quite had the motivation to stat like taking a dancing class, going rock climbing or joining a free running group.

The point of this method is to get individuals out of the house and put them in unfamiliar situations that often require socializing (sometimes with strangers in the beginning, but with the potential to become new friends). By giving people something else to focus on and also a solid means of using up manic energy, picking up a new habit or starting a new routine is one of the most trusted and proven methods of beating overthinking habits and replacing them with something that carries its own benefits for any person's physical, emotional and mental health.

Invest in A Timer & Start Settings Limits for Yourself

One step overthinkers can take in an effort to overcome the negative effects connected to the habit is to go to the store and pick up a timer or download a timer app on your phone (if it does not have one already). This method has proven the most effective for those who have struggled with conquering their habitual overthinking with more direct efforts in the past without any success or noticeable progress.

Many psychological habits have some of the same effects as addiction. Overthinking is one of those habits. Symptoms similar to those associated with withdrawal in addicts are something that overthinkers have had to experience when they try to stop their overthinking cold turkey through distractions or denial. These individuals focus all of their mental and emotional energy on denying their thoughts or distracting themselves when negative overthinking takes over their mind. There is no positive effect associated with this type of denial and that it only serves to make the overthinking worse by making the habit and not caving to it all that they can think about. Obsessing about overthinking is just as damaging and dangerous to a person's mental, emotional and physical health as habitual overthinking itself.

Instead of trying to stop overthinking, this method allows individuals to let their overthinking run throughout their mind, but on their terms and within their chosen time frame. The first step in this practice is to find a timer. Once that has been done, the person needs to decide how long they want to devote to their overthinking habit.

- This can be based on a certain amount of time per day or it can be determined by the urgency or severity of the specific task, action or event that they have been overthinking about.
    - For example, if someone struggles with habitual overthinking every time they lay down or have a moment of quiet time then they will most likely want to schedule their overthinking sessions for a set amount of time each day before bed or earlier in the

day so that they are less likely to think about it before bed. If someone is just overthinking about a certain event or action that has happened recently or is in the process of happening, they may want to pick a larger window of free time in which they can schedule an overthinking session.

- More than anything, the benefit of this method is that it helps the individual putting it into practice weaken their overthinking habit by breaking it out of its regular time frame (before bed or during shower time, whenever the person faces it the most frequently) and giving the person the power to choose when they will let their overthinking run free so they can better focus on what they should be doing and thinking about outside of that time frame.
- If you find yourself needing to dedicate time to thinking about something you are worried will turn into an overthinking session, then it is fine to schedule one that you were not expecting. In these types of situations, the most important part is to make sure you stick to your set time limit whether it is five minutes or an hour. Once you schedule an unexpected

overthinking session and then do not stick to the time limit, the habit has control over your thoughts, actions and behaviors again and the individual has taken a step backwards in their progress.

One of the main reasons this method has proven to be so effective for a variety of men and women is that is easy to adapt to nearly any schedule and can be altered and arranged when unexpected life events pop up and interfere with previously laid plans or pop up and upset the emotional state of the person and those around them.

Change the Way You Think: Gratitude Vs Regret

One issue that the majority of overthinkers struggle with is thinking about the past (recent events or situations that happened years ago) and replaying their words and actions or inability to react through their mind. These overthinking sessions fill the person's mind with thoughts of what they should have said or done or that they should have walked away from something negative instead of getting involved and making the situation worse for themselves. There will always be things in the past that people want to forget about or wish they could have done better, but as we discussed earlier, there is no way to predict the future or change the past.

This is where overthinkers need to abandon their regrets, releasing them from their thoughts and trying to move forward in a more positive lifestyle path. Once they are willing to let go of these negative thoughts and emotions, they can be replaced with a more positive way of thinking that will help people not only break their overthinking habit but also improve the way they see the world around them.

Gratitude is the opposite of regret. Knowing this, people who use this technique in order to overcome their habitual overthinking start by making a list of everything in their life that they are grateful for. It could be the basics like their family, friends and other loved ones or be related to the situation currently inspiring their overthinking habit like being grateful for their being employed when difficulties at work are causing stress and panic within their personal emotions, thoughts and behaviors. Once a person is able to see in writing or digitally on a phone or computer screen in front of them all the good and positive influences in their life that they are grateful for, it is easier to push away those negative repetitive thoughts that are most powerful during times of overthinking.

People who know why they should be grateful and what they have that they are grateful for, it is easier to take a more positive view of the world around them be it at work or in their personal life. Some people recommend carrying their list in a jacket pocket, purse or wallet. If the list was done virtually then keeping a screenshot or copy of it saved on their phone or tablet, anywhere that it is easily accessible, no matter where they are, has proven to be the most helpful and most recommended technique for achieving success with this method.

How to Stop Overthinking

1. Write it down
2. Plan a time to think about it
3. Allow yourself 15 minutes to think about it

Think & Act with Confidence: Stop Asking "What If"?

Obsessing over what could have been or what could be is counterproductive for everyone who is trying to live more in the moment or find practical means of reaching their goals. While hypothetical situations can be beneficial in certain situations, when they start to become all that a person can think about whenever faced with a task or challenge then it has reached a point of being out of control that is damaging to their personal health.

The best way to stop focusing on the potential options and start taking control of your present situation is to practice being more self-aware of your thoughts and impulses when you realize you are starting to get lost in a whirlwind of hypotheticals. When individuals notice that they are stuck in a cycle of "what ifs", the best course of action is to change their thinking from the emotional, fearful and panic-driven to the rational. Most people who practice this method take a step back to analyze their current thoughts or whatever concern is causing them to overthink in terms of the Big Picture.

Once this is done and they have taken a moment to calm their dominant emotions, the next step is to take their improved understanding of the situation and make a list of pros and cons or risks and benefits, the specifics of the list or chart will depend on what works best for the situation. The purpose of this is not just to make a list and get their thoughts organized, but to give the person a collection of practical reasons why or why not they should be doing something. Those practical reasons help them to make a logical and reasonable decision based on productive thinking instead of an impulsive course of action inspired by fear or other strong emotion.

Ask for Help: Reach Out to the People Who Love You & Build A Network of Support Around You

No one is strongest when they are on their own, despite what the anti-social and aggressive personality types may try to argue about it. Like with any psychological habit or negative behavior, people have a better chance of conquering it if they let others know what they are doing and recruit people to join their fight and help hold them responsible. By building a support network of people who love them and want to see them succeed, people are better able to stick to the goals they create for themselves and also have a security net to help keep the focused, motivated and on track on days when the person feels low or is less interested in what their mind is doing than just using their overthinking habit as a way to escape their current problems and concerns.

This can be difficult for those who have difficulty communicating with others about their feelings, thoughts or concerns. However, studies have shown that those who have people holding them accountable and those who swallow their pride and ask for help have higher success rates in all aspects of their life than those who bottle their emotions and separate themselves from people who could boost their spirits and encourage them when they are feeling down.

The Music Method: Take Control of Thoughts by Turning to Your Favorite Tunes

The part of the brain that fuels habitual overthinking and the part that is most active when a person is enjoying music are separate areas that do not actively function at the same time. What this means for people who are trying to defeat their impulses to overthink about things is that with this method, they stand their best chances of taking control of their thoughts and emotions by plugging in their headphones and getting lost in their favorite songs, channels or stations.

Music has a strong connection to a person's emotional state and can affect the way a person feels in the moment or even boost the brain's overall performance! There have been countless studies done on the effects of classical music on the brain with most of them showing an improvement in total understanding, thought processing, creativity and the absorption and processing of newly learned information. If someone is trying to stop their overthinking using the Music Method, then the first step is to become aware of their current emotional status and their emotions connected to the concern or issue that is causing their overthinking. Once that emotion (or collection of emotions) has been identified, the next step is to choose songs, styles or artists that inspire the opposite emotions in you when you let go of stress and allow yourself to get lost in the sounds.

For example:

- If someone is feeling depressed and saddened by past events that are continuously playing through their thoughts, then they should choose music that makes them smile or relaxes them. Maybe the songs they choose are once that affect them not only emotionally but physically, making them want to dance or sway, maybe run or go for a walk around the neighborhood Anything to just get their blood pumping in some way or another.
- If someone is overwhelmed by the number of disconnected or distracted thoughts running around their mind during their current overthinking session, then they should put on some music that relaxes their mind and body. The beat should be slower or more gentle and should help steady the person's heart so that they feel more calm and in control while they listen to it.

Whatever the reason they are panicked and trapped in a negative cycle of habitual overthinking, as long as they choose music that inspires an equally strong but opposite reaction in their mind or body, they will be able to break their repetitive and damaging thoughts in place of a more favorable emotional state in which rational thoughts can make themselves known.

Meditation & Mantras: There's No Limit to Their Usefulness!

These techniques have a habit of showing up on just about any self-help call to action or to-do list. As over-published and talked about as some people claim they are, there is a reason for their popularity and widespread appeal: they work for just about anything they are put to use for!

Meditation is a mental and spiritual exercise that helps individuals become more aware of their physical, mental and emotional state in order to better understand themselves as a whole. The ultimate impact of a meditation session is different from person to person depending on their specific concerns and the task or goal they are trying to reach. There are hundreds of free meditation tracks available on sites like YouTube for no cost at all and a wide range of meditation apps and channels available for free or subscription throughout the internet and in the app stores.

For those who are not interested or have not had any noticeable progress with practices like meditation or for those who want to personalize their meditation experience, creating a personal mantra is a great first step! Many overthinkers trying to regain control over their mind and emotions have seen amazing success with mantras.

Mantras are a short statement, phrase or question that a person repeats (mentally or out loud) repetitively in order to inspire a change of emotion or a break in a certain cycle of thinking. The repetition of this personal statement is intended to reinforce something that the person is hoping to achieve or something they need to remind themselves in an attempt to stay motivated or improve a stressed or depressed mood that is negatively affecting their thoughts or behaviors.

The best mantras are those that address or are connected to the struggle an individual is trying to get a handle on. Examples of simple but powerful mantras that also have a wide range of uses include:

- I believe, I can.
- Breathe in. Exhale.

- Get up. Just move.
- Let it go. Release.

These are just simple ones that address some of the most common causes and triggers behind overthinking in men and women of all ages. If none of these work for you or address your problem, then choose a phrase that does! The main reason that mantras have proven to be such a powerful tool for overthinkers looking to break their habit is that every overthinker's brain is already acting in a cyclical and repetitive manner. If a person's brain is already repeating thoughts and ideas, then why not put that behavior to good use and start to make it a productive and positive habit by repeating a phrase that strengthens them instead of damages their self-esteem or confidence in themselves?

Get Out of the House & Volunteer: Turn Your Thoughts to the Needs of Others

One of the most commonly shared traits of overthinkers is that they tend to be focused on their own thoughts, concerns and responsibilities (sometimes real but often imagined through hypothetical situations and anxious thought circling). This centralized thinking can often come across as narcissism or even pride, even though in many cases the person in question also struggles with low self-esteem or a lack of confidence.

Pro Tip: One of the key tricks anyone needs in order to master the art of building a new habit or before changing their behaviors is to become aware of their self-esteem and confidence levels. These traits create the foundation for each and every habit or personality shaping behavior that someone is hoping to start or strengthen. (This is something we will cover in further depth and detail in the next chapter).

One of the actions someone can when they are trying to overcome their damaging and habitual overthinking is to take themselves out of their familiar surroundings and change their perspective in order to get a more open and wider view of the world around them. Often times, people who try this method for conquering their overthinking find that they do not even have to travel very far, but that there are people within their own community that can benefit from volunteering efforts like feeding underprivileged families or collecting donations for the homeless community in their area. These are just some of the most popular and widely available activities that can be found in nearly any community or nearby city for those who live in smaller or more secluded areas.

The Conversational Exercise: Stretch Out All of Those Social Muscles & Skills

For those who do not have the time to get involved with a volunteer program and are searching for a smaller exercise that they can take part in whenever or wherever they may find themselves throughout the day, another popular exercise for those looking to focus on the needs of others is as follows:

1. Pick three people you have been wanting to contact or catch up with
2. Once the three people have been chosen, send each of them a message or an email letting them know that you have been thinking about them and asking about how they are. For those who are trying to be more direct with their connections and interactions, a phone call (even if it leads to a leaving a voicemail) is always a great course of action as well!
3. Give them a few days to respond before following up if you would like to, but in terms of the exercise, whether or not they respond is not important. The reason for this is because

the purpose of this exercise is to turn your thoughts to someone else when you notice yourself starting to overthink. As long as you chose three friends or family members and sent them some form of message to see how they are, you have achieved your goal and taken the first step into building a positive habit of changing the way your mind works when you start to habitually and compulsively overthink.

Alternately, you can choose three strangers, co-workers or others you may encounter throughout the day and start a conversation with them, making sure to ask about their current life status, events you know have recently happened or that they are preparing for, or just if there is anything they need to talk about. If you are uncomfortable bringing up sensitive or emotional subjects with people you have just met or do not know very well, then go ahead and start a conversation with lighter topics such as weekend plans or movies they are interested in seeing, following after whatever comes up or whatever course the conversation naturally takes. The key to making the exercise work in situations like this is to just make sure the conversation stays focused on the person you are speaking with and their concerns.

Why This Exercise Works: This method and exercise are effective because they encourage the individual putting them to use to become more active in their community and more social with the people they encounter daily. In some cases, people have even been able to reconnect with friends or family members that they had strained relationships with or lost contact with years before. Even if the message ends up going nowhere, the person has made steps toward building a positive social habit to replace their habitual overthinking. This exercise teaches people through stress-free experience that it is okay to make the first move when it comes to speaking to other people and helps with building confidence over time, helping people to become more bold with their actions or voicing their opinions in personal and professional situations.

Who This Exercise Works Best For: This method and exercise are most effective for anyone who is wanting to expand their social skills or just their social circle, anyone who is trying to overcome their habitual overthinking, anyone who is trying to build their confidence levels and anyone who is trying to gain new skills and train their brain to be more positive when it comes to interacting with other people.

Regardless of where a person's anxieties and habitual overthinking come from, there is always a way to expand their emotional intelligence, understand their personal factors and variables and make a plan of action that will help them see the most progress with practice and better control over time!

Chapter 6: Confidence is Key When It Comes to Building Positive Habits

There is a strong connection between confidence, emotional control and the conquering of psychological habits. Over the years, through all of the surveys, interviews and studies conducted, this is the most common and repeated truth from those participating in them and those performing them: no matter what a person is trying to attempt, confidence is key!

There are lots of different life factors that can affect a person's self-esteem and confidence with adolescence taking the largest toll on a person's view of themselves. During adolescence, humans It is in these years that men and women receive the majority of their emotional education as it has the highest inclusion of factors like the following for most people:

- First romantic relationships (often tumultuous with lots of highs and lows)
- First deep friendships that are tested by adjusting hormones, changing personalities

and other life factors that may arise without warning
- First major successes and accomplishments like national awards and recognition, college scholarships and summer internships
- Learning to drive and understanding the responsibility that comes with getting behind the wheel of a car
- Developing decision-making skills that are shaped by how adolescents handle things like peer pressure, balancing their school, work and social lives, and making their first life-affecting decisions like if they want to further their education after their required schooling is completed

With all of these exciting changes taking place, how could someone's self-esteem and confidence levels be hindered or even damaged? Unfortunately, for all of the positive events men and women experience during their teenage years, there are also a lot of negative events and factors they face (in their highest quantity and intensity than most people see throughout the rest of their lives) such as:

- Learning to differentiate affectionate teasing from friends and loved ones with harmful teasing and bullying that comes from those with the intention to cause harm
- Physical changes to their skin, muscles and other parts of the body that may require attention from over-the-counter medical products or even prescriptions from medical professionals
- Emotional changes that are often unexpected and out of control as skills are developed through experience and education
- Lots of fear and uncertainty as everything seems to be changing around them without a sense of direction or stopping point in sight

Not everyone has come out of adolescence with more negative memories than positive ones, but for those that did and find those negative experiences or memories affecting their adult lives, never fear! There is always action that can be taken to improve your self-esteem and confidence levels in order to improve your overall life satisfaction and path to reaching your goals!

Self-Esteem & Confidence Levels: How Are They Connected & How Are They Different?

Many times, when people talk about self-esteem and confidence, they speak about them as if they are one and the same. However, in truth, self-esteem and confidence are two separate personality traits that are often interconnected but can be damaged or weakened on their own and need individualized attention in order to help rebuild and strengthen them.

Pro Tip: Self-awareness is one of the skills people should try to master or at least become more familiar and practiced at before turning their energies to self-esteem and confidence. Without knowing where you stand psychologically, mentally and emotionally, it is difficult to determine where your focus should be aimed and what kinds of goals you should set to reach your ultimate hopes and aspirations.

A Self-Awareness Exercise: Listen to Your Self Talk & Learn from What You Say

One of the best ways for someone to understand their emotional status and why they are feeling a certain way about something is to listen to how they are speaking to themselves, either vocally or in their mind. Everyone has a little voice in their thoughts that voices their opinions about what they are thinking or what they are doing in a way that is honest, even if sometimes it can be discouraging or even cruel. The reason this voice can be trusted as a person's most honest thoughts is because these are the thoughts, ideas and opinions that only circle through someone's mind when they are alone (especially if they are voiced audibly) or whenever they have the opportunity (for those who play the voice in their minds where only they ever hear them).

Those with lower self-esteem and confidence levels often find that their private voice is a negative one, repeating Self Talk that further damages their view of themselves or opinion of their abilities. For this exercise, the goal is to teach individuals how to be more aware of this Self Talk and its tone so that they know how to change their current thought process or emotional status any time their Self Talk takes a negative turn.

- When you feel yourself inner voice becoming negative, whether this is because you are unsatisfied with something about your physical appearance or because of a broken sentence in an earlier social interaction, it will start to make critical comments or try to target other fragile or underdeveloped aspects of your personality in order to bring your mood further down.

- o Self-depreciation and attacks on one's own status or abilities are some of the most damaging behaviors someone can take part in and in many cases, this voice develops subconsciously, only voicing fears and concerns when the brain knows the person is emotionally vulnerable.
- When this behavior starts to take over your thoughts, take a step back and calm your mind. Listen to those thoughts and how your inner voice sounds (or your vocal tone) when the Self Talk starts.
  - o What kind of tone does your voice or inner voice take?
    - Is it angry, sad or hurtful?
    - Does it express any kind of emotion or does it come across as a more neutral side to your character?

- What kind of words is that voice using?
  - Are they offensive?
  - Are they words you do not normally use when talking to other people?
- When is this voice most active?
  - Does the Self Talk get most negative or most targeted during times of stress? Or any time you are not thinking about something else?
  - Do your own thoughts, actions and behaviors determine how active the voice is? Or is it more active after encounters with others?

Why This Exercise Works: This exercise works because it is based around a natural human behavior that all men and women have in common, an inner voice that takes charge of conveying our deepest and most private thoughts about the things we do and say each day. When regularly practiced, it has proven to be one of the most effective exercises in helping people expand their emotional intelligence and their understanding of themselves and how they view their private thoughts.

Who This Exercise Works Best For: This exercise has proven the most effective for those who are dedicated and motivated to take control of their emotional and psychological health. Anyone who is ready to better understand who they are and what makes them tick in order to improve their interactions with others or saying yes to more opportunities will also see noticeable progress when this exercise becomes habit and makes its way into their daily routine.

Once a person becomes comfortable with self-awareness habits and has a better understanding of where their emotional health is, they are better able to make an actionable plan for how to first improve their self-esteem and confidence levels before moving on to more stubborn and difficult to break psychological habits like compulsive overthinking and procrastination. But what is self-esteem and why is it such an important element to master when it comes to expanding emotional knowledge and health?

What Is Self-Esteem?

Self-esteem is most commonly defined as how a person feels about themselves as a whole. There is often an emotional connection to a person's self-esteem that is not shared with someone's confidence levels.

This trait is one that covers how an individual may feel about:

- Their current life status
- Their current job status
- Their relationship status
- Their main hopes and how they are working toward them
- The people around them like friends and family
- Their physical strengths and where they want to work more

These are just some of the individual factors and variables that can go into shaping a person's view of themselves and their self-esteem. If everyone in the world made a list of the points and traits they think about when they think about their view of themselves, you would most likely see a lot of repeated important factors. However, another certainty that many experts and professionals who study the effects of self-esteem on people is that there will also be as many differences as there are similarities. The reason for this is that everyone has different values or expectations for themselves based on an additional variety of factors such as:

- The environment they were raised in
- The family values instilled in them throughout childhood
- Their personal beliefs and values that have developed throughout their individual life experiences
- The expectations they set and the standards they hold themselves and those around them

These are just some of those additional factors that can help to shape an individual. The more in-depth someone looks into their own thoughts, feelings, ideas, hopes and dreams, the more they will know about themselves and the higher their self-esteem will grow to be.

Where It Comes From: A person's self-esteem is most commonly shaped by their emotional experiences and encounters. The mistakes, triumphs, accidents and successes that come throughout life all carry their own emotional and psychological influences with them. It's these influences that are most powerful when it comes to shaping how a person views themselves and their current lifestyle or life situation. The more positive influences and experiences a person is able to collect, the better their self-esteem will be and the more emotionally in control they will find themselves when stressful situations arise.

What Is Confidence (or Self-Confidence)?

Confidence (particularly when described as self-confidence) refers to faith a person has in their own knowledge, experience, skills and abilities. Depending on how much belief someone has in the things they know, the things they say, and the things they do during their personal or professional interactions, the higher a person's confidence levels will be.

Where It Comes From: A person's confidence comes from their opinion of and trust in their own strengths and abilities. This trust and faith most often are the result of positive experiences such as promotions at work or awards at school. The more experience they have and proof they have been able to collect that they know what they are doing or what they are talking about, then the higher their self-confidence will be and the more that will start to positively affect other areas of their life.

There are lots of people who have a high level of self-esteem but find that they lack confidence, especially in certain situations like when they are asked to do something without time to prepare or when they want to ask a question, but are concerned with how others will react to it so they decide to just keep their hand down. Alternately, people may have high levels of self-confidence and belief in their personal abilities, but also have poor levels of self-esteem from having their heart broken in a failed relationship or from trust issues that developed after being double-crossed by a friend or a co-worker.

Why Are These Traits So Important for Men & Women to Embrace, Develop & Strengthen?

As different as they can be, there are also plenty of situations and experiences that can be caused by interconnected levels of self-esteem and confidence. The more understanding, experienced and control a person has over their personal self-esteem and confidence levels, the better off they will be in all opportunities they attempt or goals they strive for throughout their life.

Strengthening these traits not only helps with improving a person's overall mental, psychological and emotional health, but it also comes with a variety of other benefits that can help improve someone's personal health and wellness in a wide range of styles.

The Many Benefits of Building Self-Esteem & Confidence

Even for those who are happy with their control over their habitual overthinking and procrastination, there are an endless number of reasons to keep focused on and motivated to work on for anyone and everyone building self-esteem and confidence levels. Here is a look at some of the most popular and widely reported benefits people have experienced in their quests for higher self-esteem and confidence!

- Those with higher self-esteem and personal confidence are less likely to be people pleasers or develop people pleasing habits than those with lower opinions of themselves or their abilities
- They also tend to have better performance ratings and higher success rates in leadership roles
    - Not only are they more personable with customers or other audiences, but they are also more empathetic with employers or co-workers and better able to boost morale during times of high demand or increased stress levels

- They are also more likely to have higher success rates with setting and reaching personal and professional goals because they are more self-aware of their mental, psychological an emotional changes and how it affects their daily performance
- Those with higher self-esteem and confidence levels report more personal and professional satisfaction throughout the course of their lives
  - They are more likely to take up opportunities when offered
  - They also tend to be bolder and more dominant in their professional teams and social circles as they are more likely to openly share their opinions and start conversations with even those they do not know with more confidence than those who question themselves and hesitate around others

These are just a handful of the benefits that study and research subjects of all ages and lifestyles have reported when tracked over time and throughout the course of their personal improvement journey! Each person will find a whole new array of benefits and progress markers that are specialized and more tailored to their individual needs based on the techniques they choose to put into practice, how dedicated they are able to remain to their self-improvement plan and of course, what specific issues and concerns that are working to improve or eliminate.

How to Get Started with Building Self-Esteem & Confidence Levels

Like with developing any new positive habits to replace the damaging negative ones, the first step to getting started revolves around a person's self-awareness of their thoughts and emotions. The first thing anyone should do when trying to build their self-confidence and self-esteem is to take a look at their points of strength and points of concern. The following is an example of a self-awareness exercise that many people have reported progress with during their own quests for higher self-esteem.

A Self-Awareness Exercise: Get to Know Yourself & Your Restrictions

This self-awareness exercise is one f the most basic, one of the most widely used and one of the most effective, proven techniques for anyone trying to get a better idea of their personal highs and points where they may want to work on improving in order to make the most of their personal potential.

- Set aside a time where you can clear your mind and focus on the concerns at hand
    - Make sure to deal with any potential distractions such as silencing your cell phone and turning off your television, perhaps even closing the door to the room you are going to be contemplating in so that you are not interrupted by anyone else in the building
- Lay out a clean piece of paper and get the kind of pens that you when working on organizational thinking
    - For some, they may just use a basic blue or black pen for anything they need to write, but when it comes to organization, some people prefer multiple colors or types of tips to choose from in order to separate different thoughts, ideas or options into color-coded or differently shaped areas

- Make a list of your strengths
    - This can be emotional strengths like being able to remain calm in high stress situations or always responding to friends and family the same day they message you
    - This can be professional strengths like mastering a certain skill or getting recognition for something you accomplished in your department
    - This can be personal strengths like organization and discipline, anything that you take pride in and use on a regular basis
- Now flip the paper over or draw a line to separate your lists and make a list of your weaker points or skills that you want to develop and master
    - Again, these points can be emotional like a tendency to breakdown when challenges arise in your personal or professional life
    - They can be professional points of concern like wanting to be better at communicating with customers or being

bolder when it comes to discussing a promotion with your employer
- They can also be personal, like a bad habit snapping at people who speak to you early in the morning or late in the day

- You do not have to make lists!
  - Some people find that this exercise works better when they form connecting circles of related thoughts or pie charts of strengths, weaknesses and action plans
  - The point is not to force your mind to start thinking in lists, but rather to find a way to organize your thoughts related to personal strengths, weaknesses and goals for self-improvement

Why This Exercise Works: This exercise has proven so effective for a variety of different personality types and characters because it can be tailored to work for any individual's particular way of thinking. Unlike most of the exercises and methods for overcoming negative psychological habits, this exercise does not require the person involved to change their mind or their thought processes, but rather can be altered and specialized in order to work best for their particular way of organizing their thoughts.

Who This Exercise Works Best For: Thanks to its ability to be altered and shaped to be an effective tool for nearly anybody, this exercise and those who strongly support its benefits can easily claim to work best for anyone who is willing to give it a try. Those who have been searching for a way to better understand themselves and learn about where their personal restrictions come from will also find this exercise to be a powerful tool. Mainly, anyone who is hoping to expand their self-awareness and be honest with themselves about points of weakness they fear or try to ignore will find this exercise to be not only helpful and informational, but illuminating and even may serve as a source of inspiration for those who have been trying to get motivated into self-improvement for some time without success.

Confidence Building Tip: Fake It Until You Make It

Often associated with Hollywood movie stars, this quote, *fake it until you make it*, is another popular saying that is being shared around social media support groups and self-improvement classes around the world. The basic meaning of this phrase is that if someone wants to build their confidence, all they need to do is project an air of confidence in everything they do, or pretend to be more confident than they feel when confronted and in time, this will become habit. Once someone is in the habit of pretending to be confident, this practice becomes their instinct and begins to feel natural in situations where the individual has been practicing their self-confidence building skills through faking it until they make it.

There are some people who do not like talking about building their confidence or projecting an air of confidence whenever they tackle a challenge! It makes them feel selfish and desperate for attention due to negative experiences with being open about their lack of confidence with others (most likely toxic people) in the past. For other individuals, they avoid the subject because they have learned to connect self-confidence with arrogance or other negative emotions that people feel around those people that make confidence seem like a negative quality.

Habitual overconfidence is one of the biggest causes of these negative attachments. Overconfidence is an unhealthy emotion based in delusion where someone is bold, arrogant and sometimes even aggressive in voicing their opinions despite not having any knowledge or experience with a topic. Self-confidence is not the same thing for those who struggle with this concern. Self-confidence is based on a person's view of their own abilities and how much trust they have in them. It has nothing to do with negativity or delusional behaviors and actions that affect other people and their opinion of a person.

Check Who Is Around You: Surround Yourself with Positive People

"Toxic person" is a popular phrase in virtual circles with people who are taking a step back to take a wider and more detailed view of their life and the people they come in contact with each day. Someone who is described as *toxic* is typically someone who, through their behaviors, opinions or actions, is having a negative effect on the people around them.

- They could be someone who pretends to be the individual's friend only to take advantage of them without gratitude or to the point of harming them
- They could be someone who smiles in front of people only to speak negatively about them or making up falsehoods about them when their back is turned
- They could be someone who criticizes their friends whenever they are having a bad day so that the people around them are always feeling as badly as they are

How to Identify A Toxic Connection or Relationship

The first step to breaking out of any toxic relationship is to identify the signs around you, acknowledge and then accept them as a truth that is negative to your health and needs to be amended. Everyone's relationships are different, but here is a closer look at some of the most common signs connection to toxic relationships:

- Emotional manipulation is one sign that is prominent in any kind of toxic relationship or connection
    - The definition of this symptom varies because it can include a wide range of actions and behaviors that vary from case to case
    - At its core though, emotional manipulation refers to the intentional alteration of behaviors or way of speaking in order to avoid or manage the emotions of someone else
        - In the case of the toxic person, this can refer to an intentional intensification of tense emotions and responses when their friend or partner is talking in order to get them to leave the room or feel powerless in their current situation
        - In the case of the victim, they know that when their friend or partner is in this mood that their tense emotions will only intensify if they try to talk to them so instead they intentionally find something to

do in a different room to avoid talking to their friend or partner until they are in a better headspace
- Isolating oneself from other close connections with family or friends to spend more time with their toxic friend or partner
    - In many cases, this isolation is directly linked to and even the result of their friends and family seeing the way their loved one has changed in this relationship or connection and confronted them about it
    - This confrontation is seen as an act of aggression by the individual and they get defensive, siding with their toxic friend or partner and hindering their relationship with their supportive loved one
- Being dismissed as overly emotional or overreacting to things whenever you voice your feelings or opinions (particularly if they are counter to the toxic friend or partner)
    - In some cases, the individual is not dismissed but rather teased and ridiculed making them feel even worse about speaking their mind

- They can be accused of imaging problems that do not exist if there is an issue the toxic friend or partner does not want to deal with
- Some toxic partners might try to make the individual feel selfish or guilty if their thoughts, opinions or desires are centered around anything they need or want

- A variety of controlling behaviors have been associated with toxic relationships and connections
    - Calling a person names and speaking with a sarcastic tone in situations where it is inappropriate or hurtful
    - Endless and harmful criticism that is meant to damage their self-esteem and confidence so that they are easier to control and manipulate
    - Using intimidation and fear tactics when the person becomes too bold or exploratory for their liking
    - Blaming the person from things they had no control over or were not even connected to and throwing out

unnecessary accusations in an attempt to make their partner feel guilty about something that may not even have happened

Whatever the specifics are with toxic people, they are unhealthy influences on men and women of any age or profession. The more toxic people that are around and the longer or more connected their relationship with the individual becomes, the more power and negative influence they will have on the person. These types of relationships are often neglectful and even dangerous, and they can be some of the most difficult to break free from.

Tips & Techniques for Shaking Toxic Relationships from Your Life

It is not something that everyone gets experience with or training for early in life, but most people find themselves with at least one toxic connection throughout their adult life. This may be with a friend or co-worker, with a family member or with a romantic partner, but regardless of the specifics and the intensity, every person needs to remember that they deserve better and that as hard as at may be to cut ties, the rewards will be well-worth the effort. One thing that people who are free of toxic connections have in common is higher levels of confidence and self-esteem than those who do not have the self-awareness, knowledge, support or motivation to end toxic relationships before they take their negative tolls.

Here is a closer look at some tips, tricks and techniques from those who have successfully ended toxic connections and wanted to share their experience in order to help others do the same:

- Focus on how you need to do in order to not be as dependent on the toxic friend or partner
    - Do you need to build your self-esteem and confidence before confronting the person?
    - Should you confront the toxic friend or partner, or would it be better to just leave?
- What do you need in order to successfully end this relationship or connection without guilt or excessive stress?

- o Do you need to save up some money in order to move your things or find a place of your own?
- o Do you need to have someone come stay with you to help with emotional support and strength?
- Do not get distracted by each and every step you need to take
  - o While it is important to know what you need to do in order to make an effective plan of action, getting hooked on every little detail can serve to only increase a person's stress levels and hold them back from reaching their freedom
  - o Instead, people trying to rid themselves of toxic relationships and connections should focus on their solution and their goals in order to keep themselves motivated and looking toward the future when things start to get tough

For those who have been able to break free from their toxic friendships and other connections, the next step is to fill that void left in your social life with positive influences, new friends and relationships that will help to strengthen your emotional control, self-awareness and self-esteem over time. We have already spoken about the importance of building a supportive network of people who you trust and respect the opinion of who are willing to help you on your quest for self-improvement. This advice, above all other recommendations and tips, is repeated and shared the most by those who with experience in identifying toxic people and clearing them from their lives.

Improve Your Own Self-Esteem by Helping Others Build Their Own

One positive habit people trying to improve their self-esteem and overall confidence levels like to talk about is the practice of improving their own mood, attitude and emotional status by helping others feel better about themselves. The reason for this is simple: Spread positivity and it spreads like fire! Positivity, positive comments and vibrant emotions are all just as contagious as negativity can be, it is just a matter of people being able to embrace it, even on difficult or painful days, and share with the people you come in contact with.

There are any number of ways to accomplish this as well, so that anyone can find a way that works for them and their personality type!

- Set a goal to hand out three to five compliments to other people every day
    - Not only does this make the people you come into contact with smile and feel better about themselves, but it also helps improve the individual's confidence by encouraging conversations throughout the day that they may not have attempted if they did not have a goal they were trying to meet
    - With practice and over time, this technique becomes habit and individuals find that they are viewing the whole world around them in a more positive light and feeling better about themselves and others in general
- Set a goal to hand out three to five compliments to yourself every day
    - As important as it is to help others feel better (both for their personal self-esteem growth and your own) it is also

important to start looking at yourself in a positive light
- By picking out three to five things each day that you are proud of yourself for or that you are pleased with about your appearance, behaviors or interactions, you are directly boosting your own self-esteem and confidence
- Being more positive to yourself also makes it easier to feel more confident in social situations where an individual may have previously had difficulty becoming active or connecting with others

- Do you love cooking or baking? Surprise your friends, family or co-workers with a new recipe you have been meaning to try but may not have had the opportunity!
    - Not only is this a chance to make others smile, but it also provides a fun opportunity to reach a goal you have perhaps been procrastinating in a way that boosts both your confidence and the positive mood of the people around you
    - This also provides an opportunity to open lines of conversation with people that you

may have been wanting to speak with but have not been sure how to approach
- Acknowledge other people's accomplishments
    - Not everyone likes attention when they reach a goal or are successful in some excursion, but most people feel better about themselves and their efforts if they know others have recognized and appreciated their efforts
- Plan a fun activity with friends, family or co-workers and help everyone let loose!
    - Maybe it is a day of mini golf with your siblings or a movie day with the people from work, as long as it is something that gets people out of their familiar surroundings for a period of time and gets them doing something out of their ordinary routine
    - It does not have to be expensive or even cost anything
        - A picnic day at the local park or group walk at a local trail are also good ideas for those who want to plan something but are not sure

about the budgets of their friends, family or co-workers
- Volunteer to be a mentor, a counselor or a teacher to kids, men and women who need them in your community
    o If you have a special skill or are even just a good listener, there are plenty of community programs that provide volunteers the opportunity to connect with underprivileged individuals in their community
    o Sometimes there are coaching opportunities or community centers that need art teachers for local classes
    o It all comes down to reaching out and finding your niche!

Invest in A Journal & Create A Record of All of Your Forward Progress

Many adults who did not keep journals in their youth picture journals as something that high schoolers empty all of their emotional poems, secret crush information and angry doodles in. Those who did actually get into the habit of keeping a journal in their adolescence or even starting at a younger age may already still keep one as an adult, but if not, they are already aware of the benefits they carry on dealing with intense emotions, developing fears and painful doubts.

They do not only keep a record of negative thoughts, feelings and emotions but also the moments of pride, happy events that became positive memories, new achievements and detailed hopes or dreams for the future. The best part about looking back on all of the entries and the comments they contain is that the individual can trust that these are their truest and most honest comments. They can be certain of this because they know that they are writing each time they open their journal in thoughts and emotions that they will never have to worry about explaining to anyone else.

Here is a closer look at some of the most influential benefits men and women of all ages can take advantage of by building the habit of entering their thoughts, feelings, concerns and goals into a journal at regular intervals such as every night before bed or each morning while they are drinking their coffee, or even every other day if this is an easier schedule for them to keep and habit for them to develop.

Pro Tip: Journals are also a great place to practice the three to five compliments to yourself each day! That way you not only have a record of negative and positive fluctuations each day, but you can also look back at your previous entries or look forward to each regular entry because you know each one has at least three positive statements to help boost your self-esteem a little more every time you open the journal.

The Benefits of Keeping A Journal in Adulthood
- Keeping a journal helps adults (particularly those with difficulty expressing with or processing emotions) expand their emotional intelligence
    - One way this happens is by creating a consistent record of how their emotions have changed in the time they have been keeping the journal that the individual can look back on and learn from
    - Journals create a record of events, notable emotions or interactions, accomplishments and major regrets (all kinds of major factors that can affect how a person is feeling and controlling their thoughts, emotions and behaviors)

- Men and women who grow accustomed to honestly sharing their thoughts in written form are more confident in opening up about their thoughts and feelings in daily conversation
- Journaling has proven an effective method for people looking for ways to organize their thoughts when they fall victim to their habitual overthinking or getting themselves motivated when procrastination habits take over
    - The main reason behind this is that writing out their thoughts or concerns helps individuals to calm themselves down to a point where their rational thoughts are able to take over for in controlling their behaviors, decisions and actions than their emotional impulses or psychological habits
- People who journal about their fears and weaknesses, strengths and hopes, and actions or reactions in their present situations are better at seeing the Big Picture in any situation they need to
    - This is a valuable character skill that is common in those who hold leadership roles

- These people also work better in group situations and have more open minds than the people around them who are less empathetic or willing to accept the flaws and shortcomings of themselves, their friends, family or co-workers
- Those who journal become more confident in how they speak and how they express themselves to others
    - This is why keeping a journal is one of the most recommended and respected practices in use for those who are hoping to improve their communication skills
- Journaling can help to strengthen and even speed up the emotional healing process
    - Many people have difficulty expressing their deepest thoughts and feelings with others even when it would b the best thing for them
    - After traumas like surviving a car crash or being in some other kind of serious accident
    - Losing someone you love or being betrayed by someone you trusted

- Nearly any kind of event that leaves a psychological, emotional or even physical mark or scar can increase their chances of healing in a timely manner and without permanent damage when the individual does not bottle up their emotions
- If someone does not want to share their emotions openly with people around them, then keeping a journal can help with the processing of painful or harmful emotions and help with seeing progress made over time for those situations, accidents or traumatic events that may take more than a few months to a year to overcome

Be creative, always ask questions and never stop exploring! Even if these techniques are not suited for you, there is always a way to boost your self-esteem and confidence levels so that you reach your full potential and achieve inner peace throughout the course of your life. Reach out to others either by sharing your feelings throughout your process and quest or by sharing your successes and struggles after you have seen a noticeable change. Everyone has their private concerns and worries, and you never know who you may inspire to start bettering themselves and their lives after hearing how you have been working so hard to improve yours!

Chapter 7: Moving Forward & Staying Strong in the Face of Every Challenge

You have now read through and collected some of the most productive, effective and widely respect information available on overthinking, procrastination and everything that can cause or enflame them in men and women of all ages! Armed with all this knowledge, you hopefully now have everything you need in order to conquer your negative psychological habits, build new positive ones and start moving toward a successful life path that is full of satisfaction and self-respect.

In this final chapter, we will cover some proven and well-practiced next steps that readers can take if they find themselves getting stuck, needing motivation, still seeking answers to some specifics they have experienced that may not have been covered in our thorough and informative guide, or run into any other kind of trouble! Never forget that whenever you are in doubt or having a difficult time:

- This situation, your feelings towards it and how it is affecting you is temporary
    - Take a step back, take a deep breath and use your self-awareness skills to get a better picture of the specifics and requirements connected to the situation
- Get out and get some fresh air
    - Get your blood moving and soon your mood and emotional state will improve right behind it!
    - Remember that changing your current surroundings provides fresh perspective and can help with clearing your thoughts
- Call up your friends and make some plans!
    - Many times, overthinkers and procrastinators have lost their social connections and personal relationships to their psychological compulsions
    - Sometimes one of the best ways to encourage yourself to keep moving forward or to get back in the right mindset to keep progressing is to just swallow your fears and anxieties and reach out to the people you love

- Those who reach back are often the best people for your network of support as they already have some kind of affection or even just conversational connection with you and are happy to reconnect
- Do not let yourself get concerned about those who do not reach back after you make the first move! Just sending the first message or asking others to get involved with some social plans is a huge step to overcoming habitual overthinking and procrastination

Looking for more options or actions? Keep reading for more exercises and recommendations on how to gain control of your negative habits and become happier and more confident in yourself and your mind!

Don't Let Others Determine How You View Yourself

This issue is often directly connected to a person's level of self-esteem. How high someone's self-esteem levels may or may not be is directly connected to how positively a person sees themselves and their emotions toward their behaviors, thoughts and actions. One of the most popular quotes currently circling self-improvement groups on virtually every social media site is:

- What anyone else thinks about you is none of your business
    - The purpose of this quote is not to make anyone feel worse about themselves or about how they perceive how others see them
    - Rather, its purpose and full intent is to provide people with a way to remind themselves when they start to worry about what people around them are thinking that they are better off letting it go and turning their attention to more positive and productive thoughts
    - This is where those skills, methods and techniques that the person is putting into practice become their most powerful tools for building self-esteem and confidence levels

Those who seek the approval and affection of everyone they meet will never find their true happiness or be able to gain any control over their psychological habits. The main reason for this is that people who are constantly letting the opinion of others affect how they speak or behave never find their true selves as they constantly change to please the people around them.

Find ways to change the way your mind is thinking and practice those skills and techniques that focus on seeing things more positively and optimistically. Focus on activities that clear your mind, balance your emotions and make you more aware of who you are and what you want for yourself. This is the only way to enjoy some inner peace and live more in the moment, instead of in memory and regret or hypothetical scenarios.

Never Accept Failure & Always Plan for Success

Make changing the way your mind works to see the challenges you face and the people you encounter, even your own mind and actions, in a more positive light. That positivity, no matter where in your life it needs to be strengthened, exercised and practiced, comes with so many encouraging and inspiring benefits (mentally, emotionally, psychologically and physically as we've discussed in previous chapters) and those benefits all serve to help people reach their goals and achieve success!

Even in those situations when you are struggling to come up with a plan of action or get motivated to get moving toward a resolution, if you start your thought process under the assumption that you are going to succeed then your chances of success are already higher than they would have been if negative psychological habits like overthinking and procrastination were allowed to take over and become dominant in the brain. This goes back to the technique of faking it until you make it, or basically if you believe that you can do it you will be able to as long as you take action. The more you practice this technique, the more habitual it will become until it replaces overthinking and procrastination habits as your compulsion in times of stress or overwhelming responsibility.

As you can see in the following graph, success is not a straight line:

$$\underline{\text{Success}} \qquad \underline{\text{Success}}$$

what people think it looks like · what it really looks like

There will be times that you stumble and times that you fall. There will be tasks where you are forced to ask for help or may cave to procrastination habits due to a lack of knowledge and help or a desire to avoid a stressful situation. The trick to mastering discipline and reaching your ultimate success goals is not to keep yourself from ever falling, but rather to never accept that failing as the peak of your abilities or potential. Instead, achieving success is about giving up the quest for perfection by understanding that everyone (including you) makes mistakes throughout the course of their life and always picking yourself back up when you are down, falling or hitting the ground.

If You Cannot Make A Solid Decision, Don't Be Afraid to Play Devil's Advocate with Yourself

Devil's Advocate is a hypothetical exercise that has a long history of use and success, particularly in political, judgment matters and throughout the business world. Often sold as a strategic thinking exercise, the purpose of Devil's Advocate is to teach the user how to see opposing viewpoints to their main point or opinion.

Before Devil's Advocate can be an effective tool for forming and developing strategic thinking skills and strengthening one's own arguments or theories, the person must first be strong in their understanding and development of their own thoughts and opinions on the topic. Without that certainty and confidence, there is no way someone will be able to defend their opinion or idea against someone who is questioning them (even is that someone is themselves).

How to play Devil's Advocate:

1. Know your thought, opinion or argument with total confidence
    - Use whatever organization techniques that work for you until you are certain that your piece can stan up to criticism

2. Lay out your information as if you were your target audience
    - This can be done literally by laying out note cards or showing posters or graphs that have been created for the presentation or argument
    - This can also be done by simply performing your sales pitch or argument in a mirror so that you can gain experience in delivering it to an audience while also presenting it as if a member of that audience
3. Once that is done, take a step back and clear your mind
    - Try to look at your notes or graphics objectively
    - If you find yourself unable to look objectively at one aspect, look at your notes or presentation again and start asking "why?" every time you go back over a point
4. Question everything, even if you already know the answer (especially if you know the answer)
    - The purpose of this exercise is to search for weaknesses or flaws in an argument

or presentation in order to fix them before the event itself, thereby strengthening your stance and your delivery before anyone else ever even sees it!

Why This Exercise Works: This exercise works by opening the individual's mind to other possibilities or alternatives that they could not see or were unwilling to see from their original thought process or stance. One of the main benefits that come with practicing this exercise is that it helps with building decision-making skills for those who have difficulty with anxiety or overcoming their compulsive behaviors. By practicing their ability to see anything from the opposite or even a more neutral point of view, people who regularly play Devil's Advocate have been proven to be more empathic in their interactions with others, more driven in their professional exploits and as having higher confidence and self-esteem because they are more confident in their thoughts, ideas, behaviors and actions.

Who This Exercise Works Best For: This is a popular exercise for anyone who is looking learn how to think more strategically for work or other activities where they find their thoughts limited or their ideas sluggish. Those who have to deliver sales pitches or present arguments also develop their argument and defense skills with exercises like Devil's Advocate as a way of strengthening any weak points in their pitches or arguments by putting themselves in the same mental status their customer, employer or argument rival.

Eat Right & Exercise: Turn Your Attention to Improving Your Physical Health

One of the steps people can take to feeling better about themselves and feeling more in control of their lives is to take responsibility for their physical health. For some people, this could be as simple as giving up sweets after dinner to get started but for others it may require more intense changes that could mean altering their behaviors and lifestyle. There are a number of factors that can determine what kind of changes a person needs to make in order to improve their physical health to improve their mental, emotional and psychological health for the better:

- When was the last time you went for a physical with your primary care doctor?
    - Going for an annual check-up is something that all adults should make a priority, particularly those getting closer to their middle age years when many people begin to develop health concerns related to their heart, brain and body weight
- How often do you exercise? How regularly?
    - Most doctors recommend a regular exercising routine of 45 minutes to an hour, two to three times a week at minimum to build a healthy habit and maintain a healthy physical form
    - The frequency and time frames for exercising windows should be determined by the intensity of the exercise chosen and how well the individual is able to stay dedicated to the long-term exercise plan and goals they create
- What kind of physical activity are you doing?
    - Is it something that gets your heart pumping and keeps your body temperature higher than normal for a

healthy amount of time to burn calories such as running or going for a ride on a bicycle?
- Or is it something like yoga that does not always affect a person's heart rate, but rather focuses on muscle strengthening, emotional control and balance?

Are you already exercising? Maybe it is time to look into changing your diet to improve your physical health by improving the quality or type of food you are putting in your body!

- Do you need to lose weight in order to reach a healthy goal set by you and your doctor for your age, height and personal health status?
  - Look for a diet that encourages calorie burning foods that are high in vitamins, or lower calorie foods that do not have as much fat or processed ingredients
  - Find a diet that is higher in protein and lower in carbohydrates to reduce your calorie intake that way
- Are you unsure of what kind of diet is best for your body type or health conditions?

- While there is plenty of information available about questions like these, the best bet for those who are worried about their health or have an existing health condition of any kind is to talk with their primary health care physician or make an appointment with a dietitian or nutritionist
- Give up the fake stuff and try the organic lifestyle!
    - Organic does not have to mean expensive or difficult to find
    - Fake ingredients such as processed foods and those that are packed with chemicals to ensure they can stay fresh until the end of times are not healthy options for those that are wanting to improve their diet to improve their emotional health
    - Chemical byproducts and similar ingredients have been connected to a rise in depression, anxiety, anti-social tendencies and other psychological conditions in men and women of all ages
    - Try basing your meals around what is fresh and in season in your area!

If All Else Fails, Seek Professional Help & Support!

It all goes back to not being afraid to or uncomfortable with asking for help when you need it. If you have tried and tried a variety of different methods, tip and tricks over a respectable amount of time without any forward progress or success, your best bet may be to seek out the help of a counselor or even a medically registered therapist. While some people can get control over their psychological, mental and emotional health by improving certain personality traits or thought processes, there are also a large number of people who do not start to see their largest amount of improvement until they break through their fears and anxieties around going to the doctor and seek out the help of a trained professional.

- A good first place to start (for those who are unfamiliar with medical experts or do not have any standing relationships with any kind of healthcare professionals) is to find a general healthcare practitioner, often known as a primary care or family care doctor, that you can speak to about your questions and concerns

- A primary care doctor can perform a general physical to check your overall health and also answer questions about any emotional or psychological concerns you may be facing
    - Always remember that the more open and honest you are with your doctors (even if you feel embarrassed at first), the better, more efficiently and more quickly they will be able to help you find answers and solutions
    - Never worry about being embarrassed when talking to any kind of medical or healthcare professional! Most likely they already have experience with just about anything you can think, with the exception being the more bizarre or extreme cases. Even then, doctors love hearing about cases they have not yet faced. Like with most professionals, doctors learn best and expand their knowledge most effectively through experience.
- If your primary care doctor does not have the experience or training necessary for your particular needs and questions, they will be

able to recommend you to other healthcare professionals in specialized areas such as psychologists to help with emotional issues or specialists in specific parts of the body for those who have physical issues that need the addressing of an expert.

Each person has their own unique struggles and that means that sometimes a technique or plan that works for one person will not work for someone else, even if their issues or concerns are similar. Never be afraid to seek out more answers when you run into trials or challenges throughout your personal journey to self-improvement! Whether that means trying new things or researching new opinions, theories and techniques that are appearing online each day as more and more psychological experts and medical professionals take an interest in habitual psychological compulsions, their dangers and how each kind of personality type or situational stress victim can best learn to overcome those impulses like overthinking and procrastination in order to improve their personal, private and professional lives.

Conclusion

Thank you for making it all the way through to the end of *Overthinking: The Fast Cure for Women and Men Who Think Too Much and Want to Stop Procrastinating!*

We sincerely hope that with this guide you were able to collect the skills you need in order to overcome your negative and damaging psychological habits like overthinking and procrastination, in favor of positive and beneficial habits that:

- Are emotionally strengthening for better control over emotional reactions
- Are encouraging and motivating during times of great stress or emotional turmoil
- Improve your ability to access and take action with rational thoughts and plans that are based on logical and calm contemplation instead of being impulsive or poorly prepared
- Inspire positive changes, effects and actions like increased physical activity, better psychological understanding and increased emotional intelligence

From this point, the next step for readers is to take what they have learned with this guide and make an action plan that is tailored to their individual needs and built towards their personal goals. Whether you are wanting to overcome overthinking, become more productive or just find a way to be more confident in your own thoughts, words and skills, this guide hopefully delivered to information you needed to get started and provided plenty of options for how to take the information from the thought stage into productive action! Whatever your personal goals may be, we hope that you found the tools you need in order to make a positive change in your life with *Overthinking: The Fast Cure for Women and Men Who Think Too Much and Want to Stop Procrastinating.*

www.ingramcontent.com/pod-product-compliance
Lightning Source LLC
Chambersburg PA
CBHW071623080526
44588CB00010B/1242